Cakes, desserts, and puddings

Amandine's recipes

Cakes, desserts, and puddings

Photography by Akiko Ida

Baking cakes at home is a pleasure we can all enjoy. This book is a collection of very easy recipes remembered with affection from my childhood in France: pure butter brioche, Swiss roll, spice cake, madeleines, yogurt cakes, and so on. Maybe you remember sampling such delicacies if you have traveled in France?

Here you will find the traditional methods, together with some special tips to help you produce the real thing, using recipes handed down from one generation to the next. With three times nothing, a little butter, some flour, and a few eggs, French mothers and grandmothers knew how to create what they wanted: langues de chat, choux pastry puffs, chocolate charlotte, tarte Tatin, pound cake, fruit cake, cherry clafouti, apple turnovers, and so on.
If you cannot get hold of the exact ingredients, you can easily replace certain items with ones from your own store cupboard. The fruit breads, tarts, and cakes all work well with good quality ingredients.

Amandine

Guide to home baking

PANS FOR ALL OCCASIONS Four or five pans are all you need to make about ninety percent of the cakes in this book—that is all! Preferably, they should be nonstick pans, to make life easier. Never use a fork or knife to release your cake from the pan. You are likely to spoil both your cake and your pan if you do.

Choosing the right pan

Keep to simple pans: one loaf pan and one round cake pan about 9 inches in diameter will be sufficient to make many delicious cakes. You can gradually acquire more sophisticated pans as you need them.

Caring for your pans

Take care never to scratch the surface with an abrasive sponge and do not use strong cleaning products. Certain nonstick pans are dishwasher proof. When you buy them they will have a label telling you if they are.

Tart pans

These can be made of ovenproof porcelain or metal and come in many shapes and sizes. Variety is the spice of life!

Baking pans

A standard baking pan can be used for clafoutis and flans. To clean off stubborn stains, put a few tablespoonfuls of bicarbonate of soda in the base and fill it two-thirds full of warm water. Put it in the oven for about twenty minutes. It will come out sparkling.

Fruit cake (bread) pans

There is a secret to a successful fruit cake: put the pan on a baking sheet on a shelf in your oven. This will prevent the base from burning during cooking and the cake will be cooked to perfection.
To see if it is cooked sufficiently, plunge a knife blade into the center; if nothing sticks to it, the cake is done.

Deep, round cake pans

The ideal diameter for most of the cakes in this book is about 9 inches. Some pans are spring-form (see opposite page)—they are generally used for homemade breads and buns. Use these pans for cheesecakes and delicate cakes that are difficult to release. Never use a spring-form pan for runny or fatty mixtures that may leak out during cooking.

Brioche pans

Used for baking brioches and Kougelhopfs. There is a wide range of such pans available in Alsace—should you go there! You can sometimes find them in old-fashioned ironmonger's shops and in specialized shops selling baking equipment.

SMALL UTENSILS Here are a few practical items that will help you succeed with your homemade pastries. They are not essential but they will serve you well.

Rolling pin

Ideal for preparing homemade pastry. Usually made of wood, there are two kinds: professional rolling pins sometimes come without handles, but they are more than 14 inches long. Not a fraction of the pastry is wasted! The more usual kind has two handles.

Cake rack

Made of stainless steel, a cake rack is the best way to let your cakes 'rest' after cooking. You could also use it for serving your cakes at the table. It lends a nostalgic air.

Brushes

Use small ones for brushing over your tarts and cakes. Those made of natural fibers are preferable. Professional equipment shops and some ironmongers sell special pastry brushes. To clean them, just hold them under running water, but do not forget to dry them.

Cookie cutters

Use these for tartlets and to give a different look to buns and cookies.

Spatulas

The ones with a rubber blade are best. They ensure that none of your mixture is wasted.

Pastry wheels

Made of wood or stainless steel, these are generally used for making ravioli. You can also use them for crafting interesting shapes with your leftover shortcrust or puff pastry. Essential for making Linzertorte (see page 122).

Piping nozzles and bags

Used for creamy or frothy mixtures. Made of fabric or nylon, the bags are flexible and respond to the slightest pressure of the finger. You need a little practice. Different shaped nozzles will enable you to decorate your cakes attractively.

Balloon whisk

The alternative to an electric beater. It is, however, more practical, being ideal for making emulsions and for folding sugar into whites of egg.
Choose a strong stainless steel version. The metal wires should be supple but firm.

rolling pins
racks
brushes
spatulas
wheels
nozzles
whisks

Flours

All-purpose flour
This is the flour commonly used for making cakes and cookies. It is a wheat flour – an ideal flour that is found everywhere.

Self-rising flour
White wheat flour to which salt and baking powder have been added.

Chestnut flour
This traditional flour used in cakes and cookies in the center of France or Corsica will give a delicious hint of chestnut flavor to your desserts.

Cornmeal
This yellow flour, low in gluten but rich in starch, is perfect for making polenta, puddings, pancakes, and certain cakes such as lemon and almond cake.

Buckwheat flour
Low in gluten, this flour is mainly used to make Breton 'galettes' and certain types of pancake.

TIP • You should always sift your flour when you make a cake to get rid of any lumps and make sure your mixture is smooth.

Different types of sugar
There are two main sorts of sugar: beet sugar and cane sugar. Both can be used in baking.
Sugar is used to sweeten desserts, but it also raises the acidity of certain fruits, colors cakes in the cooking process, lends a firm consistency to certain recipes (meringues for instance), and, of course, is used for decoration (as in royal frosting, confectioners' sugar, or spun sugar).

Granulated sugar
Coarsely ground white table sugar. Golden granulated sugar is unrefined and ideal for use in baking.

Superfine sugar
A finely ground form of refined sugar used in baking because it is quick to dissolve. Golden superfine sugar is unrefined and ideal for use in baking.

Confectioners' sugar
This white sugar, pulverized and reduced to a powder to which a little starch is added, is ideal for decorating desserts.

Vanilla sugar
If you cannot buy this ready-made you can make your own by cutting one or two vanilla beans into small lengths. Put them into a screw-topped jar with 1 lb granulated sugar and leave for a week or so. Remove the vanilla beans before using the sugar.

Soft brown sugars
These are made up of small crystals and can be light or dark in color. They are slightly more 'refined' than other brown sugars and are used in waffles, pancakes, and certain cookies. Add a little to plain yogurt or fromage frais—it tastes a lot nicer than ordinary sugar.

Colored sugars
Today, there are a large number of colored sugars in different forms. Give yourself a treat and use them to decorate your cakes.

Demerara sugar
This natural cane sugar is highly perfumed and is therefore ideal for baking, particularly fruit cakes.

Nuts
This book includes dishes made with nuts and nut derivatives. It is advisable for readers with known allergic reactions to nuts and nut derivatives, and those who may be potentially vulnerable to these allergies—such as pregnant and nursing mothers, invalids, the elderly, babies and children—to avoid dishes made with nuts and nut oils. It is also prudent to check the labels of pre-prepared ingredients for the possible inclusion of nut derivatives.

Eggs
Some recipes include raw eggs. It is not advisable to serve these dishes to very young children, pregnant women, elderly people, or anyone weakened by serious illness. Be sure that the eggs are as fresh as possible. If in any doubt, consult your doctor.

buckwheat
cornmeal
chestnut
demerara
soft brown
colored

Here are three classic pastry recipes that are quick and easy, and fun to make. They occur frequently in this book.

Shortcrust pastry

Preparation time: 10 minutes
Cooking time: 15 minutes
You can prepare this the day before.

2 cups all-purpose flour
1 pinch of salt
4 tablespoons water
1 stick butter (at room temperature), cubed
1 egg yolk
¼ cup superfine sugar

Sift the flour onto your work surface.
Pour the salt into the water to dissolve it.
Make a well in the flour and put the butter into the hollow. Rub together using your fingertips until the mixture resembles fine breadcrumbs.
Roll the pastry into a ball and then make another well. Put the egg yolk, sugar, salt, and water in the hollow. Knead the pastry as quickly as possibly, then roll it into a ball, wrap it in plastic wrap, and put it in the refrigerator for about 1 hour.

TIP • Do not knead your pastry for too long. Shortcrust pastry can be used for both sweet and savory recipes. For the latter, omit the sugar.

Sweet flan pastry

Preparation time: 10 minutes
Cooking time: 15 minutes
You can prepare this the day before.

2 cups all-purpose flour
1 stick cold butter, cubed
1 cup confectioners' sugar
2 egg yolks
1 tablespoon milk
1 pinch salt

Sift the flour onto your work surface.
Make a well in the flour and put the butter and confectioners' sugar into the hollow.
Rub together using your fingertips, then add the egg yolks, milk, and pinch of salt.
Knead the pastry until it has a sandy consistency. Then roll the pastry into a ball, wrap it in plastic wrap, and put it in the refrigerator for 2 hours.

TIP • You can flavor the pastry by adding the grated peel of a quarter of an unwaxed lemon or orange.

Sweet flan pastry with almonds

Preparation time: 10 minutes
Cooking time: 15 minutes

2 cups all-purpose flour
1 stick cold butter, cubed
1 cup ground almonds
2 egg yolks
1 tablespoon milk
1 pinch salt

Sift the flour onto your work surface.
Make a well in the flour and put the butter and almonds into the hollow.
Rub together using your fingertips, then add the egg yolks, milk, and salt.
Knead the pastry until it has a sandy consistency. Then roll the pastry into a ball, wrap it in plastic wrap, and put it in the refrigerator for 2 hours.

TIP • If you have no rolling pin, you can make mini-tartlets by putting a ball of pastry in the freezer for 30 minutes and then cutting it into slices about ⅛ inch thick.

Shortcrust pastry

Bitter orange marmalade

Preparation time: 15 minutes
Cooking time: 50 minutes

1 copper or stainless steel preserving pan
about 6 1 lb jars

12–15 unwaxed bitter oranges
1 lemon
4½ cups granulated sugar

First sterilize the jars (see TIP below).
Remove the rind from three of the oranges. Cut it
into thin strips. Heat some water in a small
saucepan. As soon as it boils, drop in the rind and
poach for two to three minutes, then remove the
rind and drain.
Squeeze the oranges and put the juice and flesh
in the preserving pan.
Squeeze the lemon and add the juice to the pan.
Add the sugar, stir once, and cook the mixture
over a moderate heat for about 30 minutes.
Next, add the drained rind and continue to cook
for another 20 minutes.
Allow to cool a little before transferring to jars.
Seal the jars.
When they are cold, store them in a cool, dry
place away from light.

Strawberry jelly

Preparation time: 30 minutes
Cooking time: 20 minutes

1 copper or stainless steel preserving pan
3–4 1 lb jars

2 lb 12 oz strawberries
3½ cups granulated sugar
juice of 1 lemon

First sterilize the jars (see TIP below).
Quickly wash the strawberries under cold running
water, remove the hulls, and drain the fruit. Put
them in a bowl with the sugar and lemon juice.
Cover with plastic wrap and leave in a cold place
overnight.
Next day, remove the strawberries from the bowl
with a slotted spoon and keep to one side. Pour
the juice into the preserving pan and boil rapidly
for 10 to 12 minutes. Regularly skim off the
foam that forms on the surface. Pour in the
strawberries and cook for about 10 minutes.
Then skim.
Put the jam into the jars immediately, close, and
seal them.
When they are cold, store them in a cool, dry
place, away from light.

TIP • Before using preserving jars, you should
wash and dry them. Then place in a pan of
boiling water for several minutes, in order to
sterilize them. Stand the jars upside down to
drain on a clean dish towel. You may also
sterilize them in your oven at 225° F for five
minutes.

Cherries in syrup

Sufficient to fill 1¾ pint jar
Preparation time: 30 minutes
Cooking time: 20 minutes

1 1¾ pint glass jar

1 lb 5 oz cherries
2 tablespoons superfine sugar
1 heaped teaspoon vanilla sugar

Quickly wash the cherries under cold running
water, drain them and remove the stalks.
Fill the jar with cherries, then pour in cold, boiled
water until it reaches halfway up the jar.
Add the superfine sugar and the vanilla sugar.
Seal the jar and sterilize it for 20 minutes in a pan
of boiling water. The jar must be completely
submerged. Leave to cool in the pan.
Store the jar in a cool, dry place away from light.
Your cherries in syrup can be kept like this for up
to a year.

Apricots in syrup

Sufficient to fill a 1¾ pint jar
Preparation time: 30 minutes
Cooking time: 20 minutes

1 1¾ pint glass jar

1 lb 14 oz apricots
2 tablespoons confectioners' sugar
1 heaped teaspoon vanilla sugar

Wash the apricots and drain. Cut them in half and
remove the pits. Break four or five pits and place
the kernels in the jar. Fill it up with the apricots.
Pour in cold, boiled water until it reaches halfway
up the jar. Add the confectioners' sugar and the
vanilla sugar.
Seal the jar and sterilize it for 20 minutes in a pan
of boiling water. The jar must be completely
submerged. Leave to cool in the pan.
Store the jar in a cool, dry place away from light.
Your apricots in syrup can be kept like this for up
to a year.

Custard

Serves 4–6
Preparation time: 5 minutes
Cooking time: 5 minutes

1 vanilla bean
4½ cups milk
8 egg yolks
1 cup superfine or granulated sugar

Split the vanilla bean in two lengthways and score it well. Pour the milk into a large, heavy-based saucepan, add the vanilla bean, and heat to simmering point.
Beat the egg yolks and the sugar in a large bowl until the mixture becomes slightly frothy and takes on a pretty cream color.
Remove the vanilla bean from the saucepan and slowly pour the warm milk onto the egg-sugar mixture, stirring all the time.
Pour the custard back into the saucepan and cook on a low heat while continuing to stir. The custard is cooked when it thickens and coats the spoon. Remove the pan from the heat and leave to cool.
Custard (also known as crème anglaise) is easy to make, but it must not be allowed to boil. If any lumps occur, you can use an electric mixer to dissolve them.

Crème brûlée

The well-known crème brûlée (literally 'burnt cream') is made from the same ingredients as custard. However, you only use 1¼ cups of milk and make up the difference with 3 cups heavy cream.
Beat the egg yolks and sugar together, then warm the milk and cream and pour them into the mixture, stirring all the time. Divide the mixture into individual ramekin dishes and bake them in the oven, in a baking pan containing boiling water, for about 20 minutes at 300° F.
Just before serving, dust the dishes with demerara sugar or soft brown sugar and put them in a baking pan surrounded by ice cubes. Heat the grill to maximum and place the ramekins and the baking pan just under the heat. Do not take your eye off it!
Serve as soon as the sugar has caramelized.

Baked custard

Use exactly the same ingredients as for custard. Beat the egg yolks and sugar until the mixture becomes slightly frothy and takes on a pretty cream color. Pour the mixture onto the warm milk, stirring all the time.
Divide the custard into individual ramekin dishes and bake in the oven, in a shallow baking pan containing boiling water, for about 20 minutes at 300° F.

Confectioner's custard (Crème pâtissière)

Serves 4–6
Preparation time: 5 minutes
Cooking time: 8 minutes

1 cup milk
½ vanilla bean split in two lengthways
2 egg yolks
3 tablespoons superfine sugar
2 tablespoons cornstarch
Pour the milk into a heavy-based pan, add the vanilla, and heat to simmering point.
Mix the egg yolks and sugar in a large bowl then add the cornstarch, stirring all the time.
Slowly pour in the warm milk and mix.
Pour the mixture into a pan and let it thicken over a low heat, stirring constantly with a wooden spoon.
Leave the crème pâtissière to cool before using it to enhance your cakes.
If you like, you can flavor your crème pâtissière with a few drops of rum or Grand Marnier.

BUTTER is, needless to say, an essential ingredient for successful home baking. Here are a few tips on how to use it.

Salted butter

You can always find salted butter in the dairy section of your supermarket. It will lend a subtle taste to all your sweet recipes. It is up to you whether you choose salted or unsalted butter, according to your taste. Certain desserts are more suited to one or the other. For example, an upside-down cake (tarte Tatin) made with salted butter is exquisite.

Use in cakes and pastries

Take your butter out of the refrigerator half an hour or an hour before you start cooking, cut it into small cubes, and leave it to reach room temperature. It will then be easy to use.

Butter cream

Butter cream is ideal for filling a Swiss roll (page 134) or a sponge cake (page 64).

Sufficient for 1 cake
Preparation time: 15 minutes
Cooking time: 5 minutes

½ cup sugar
½ cup water
2 sticks butter
5 egg yolks

Dissolve the sugar in the water to make a clear syrup.
Cream the butter to soften it, pour the syrup onto the butter, and whisk together.
Add the egg yolks, one at a time.
Flavor with vanilla, coffee, or chocolate (a few drops of vanilla extract or coffee extract will be sufficient, or 1–2 tablespoons of cocoa powder).

TIP • For a 'lighter' butter cream, whisk 3 egg whites with the sugar syrup and add to the softened butter. Do not forget the egg yolks!

Crème Chantilly

Like sweet flan pastry, homemade crème Chantilly is out of this world!

You can adjust the quantity of cream each time you make it, according to how much you need.

1 cup heavy cream
1 heaped teaspoon vanilla sugar

The cream must be very cold, so put it in the bowl in which it will be whisked and place in the coldest part of the refrigerator. Leave it there for half an hour at least.
Remove the bowl from the refrigerator and pour in the vanilla sugar.
Use an electric whisk. If yours has several speeds, increase the speed gradually. The cream will become frothy and then thicken slightly. As soon as the cream sticks to the beaters it is ready! It is important to stop at the right time, otherwise it will turn to butter.

TIP • Homemade crème Chantilly does not keep well. It should be eaten the same day or it may go off.
Use heavy rather than whipping cream as it will thicken more easily.

Red fruit coulis

You may be able to buy ready-made frozen coulis, but it is not difficult to make.
You can use all sorts of red fruit: raspberries, blackcurrants, redcurrants etc.
If you see red fruit in the market that are slightly past their best, you should buy them as they are ideal for making coulis. After washing the fruit, blend them in a food processor with superfine sugar to taste. Strain to remove the seeds.
You can easily freeze your coulis and use it when you need to.

TIP • Freeze it as ice cubes; that way, you need only thaw the right quantity.

Tea and coffee breaks

Chocolate madeleines

For a tasty alternative, replace 1 cup flour with 5 oz best-quality dark chocolate. Leave out the orange flower water.

Honey madeleines

If you have access to some good honey from a beekeeper, you should try this. Simply replace ¾ cup sugar with ¾ cup honey.
If your honey has solidified, let it melt with the butter for a few minutes. Leave out the orange flower water.

Madeleines

Serves 4–6
Preparation time: 15 minutes
Cooking time: 10 minutes

1 bun sheet

5 eggs
1 pinch of salt
1¼ sticks salted butter + ¼ stick for greasing the bun sheet
1 cup superfine sugar
8 drops of flowers of orange water
1¾ cups all-purpose flour

Preheat the oven to 350° F.
Grease the bun sheet with butter.
Break the eggs and separate the whites from the yolks. Add a pinch of salt to the whites and, using a whisk, beat them until stiff.
Melt the butter gently in a small, heavy-based saucepan.
Whisk the egg yolks with the sugar and then add the melted butter and the orange flower water.
Gradually add the beaten egg whites and the flour.
Fill each cup of the bun sheet using a spoon.
Place the sheet in the oven and cook for about 10 minutes.
Then take it out of the oven and ease the madeleines from the cups.
The madeleines can be eaten while still warm but can also be kept for a few days in an airtight container.

Coconut rock cakes

Serves 4
Preparation time: 15 minutes
Cooking time: 5 minutes

1 baking sheet lined with nonstick baking paper

1 cup grated coconut
½ cup caster sugar
2 fresh egg whites
½ teaspoon vanilla extract

Preheat the oven to 410° F.
Using your fingertips, mix together the coconut,
sugar, egg white, and vanilla extract in a bowl.
Roll into little balls of equal size in your hands and
place them on the baking sheet (if you like, you
can give them a pyramid shape like the ones you
see in bakers' shops).
Leave sufficient space between the balls to
prevent them sticking together during cooking.
Put them in the oven for 5 minutes—no longer—
then take them out and leave to cool at room
temperature.

Almond brittle

Serves 4–6
Preparation time: 10 minutes
Cooking time: 40 minutes

1 cake pan or baking sheet

2 whole eggs + 1 yolk
1 cup superfine sugar
2 tablespoons brandy
1 pinch of salt
2 sticks salted butter (at room temperature),
cubed + 1 tablespoon for greasing the pan
4 cups all-purpose flour
1 cup almonds
3 tablespoons milk

Preheat the oven to 350° F.
Grease the pan with the butter.
Mix the 2 eggs with the sugar, brandy, and salt in
a large bowl.
Add the butter and mix well.
Pour in the flour in a stream, stirring all the time.
Add the almonds.
Do not work the mixture too much and use only
the fingertips.
Spread the mixture in the pan, smoothing the
surface with a spatula. Make a criss-cross pattern
with the prongs of a fork. Mix the milk and the
egg yolk in a bowl and use this to glaze the
mixture.
Bake in the oven for 35 to 40 minutes.
Leave the brittle to cool before removing it from
the pan.

Hearth cake (Galette Saint-Pierre)

It is best if you use your hands for this recipe! It is not worth getting out your food processor. You will not even need a wooden spoon. (Re)discover the pleasure of kneading with your hands..

Serves 6
Preparation time: 15 minutes
Cooking time: 25 minutes

1 cake pan or a number of tart pans

2 cups all-purpose flour
1 teaspoon baking powder
5 egg yolks + 1 egg yolk for glazing
¾ cup superfine sugar
1 pinch of salt (if using unsalted butter)
1½ sticks salted butter (at room temperature), cubed + ¼ stick for greasing the pan(s)

Preheat the oven to 350° F.
Lightly grease the pan(s).
Mix the flour and baking powder, then sift onto a work surface or into a basin.
Make a well in the center and pour in the 5 egg yolks, sugar, and salt. Mix well with the fingertips until the mixture takes on a sandy consistency.
Then add the cubed butter to the pastry and mix again.
Put the mixture into the pan(s). Using a brush, glaze the surface with a little beaten egg yolk. Make a criss-cross pattern with the prongs of a fork.
Put in the oven for about 25 minutes.
Remove cake from the pan(s) while still warm and leave to cool on a cake rack.

Meringues

Serves 4
Preparation time: 15 minutes
Cooking time: 55 minutes

1 baking sheet lined with nonstick baking paper

2 eggs
1 small pinch of salt
2 heaped teaspoons vanilla sugar
¼ cup superfine sugar
¾ cup confectioners' sugar

Preheat the over to 300° F.
Break the eggs and separate the whites from the yolks.
Add the salt to the egg whites and beat them with your electric whisk until they form stiff peaks.
Gradually add the vanilla sugar, beating all the time. Then gradually pour in the superfine sugar and confectioners' sugar while continuing to beat.
Using 2 teaspoons, divide the mixture into small blobs, all the same size and each with a pointed tip.
Line them out on the baking sheet as you go, leaving a 1 inch space between them.
Place the baking sheet in the oven and immediately lower the temperature to 275° F.
Leave to cook slowly for 55 minutes, then gently open the oven door for a few minutes. Close the door and turn off the oven. Leave the meringues inside the oven for another hour. This will make them crunchy. You can keep them for several days in a cookie jar.

Almond squares

Serves 6
Preparation time: 20 minutes
Cooking time: 8 minutes

1 baking sheet

2 egg whites
½ cup confectioners' sugar
¼ cup all-purpose flour + 1 tablespoon to dust
the baking sheet
¼ stick salted butter, melted + 1 tablespoon
to grease the baking sheet
½ cup almonds, chopped or slivered

Preheat the oven to 410° F.
Grease the baking sheet with butter and dust
lightly with flour.
Whisk the egg whites and confectioners' sugar to
form a light frothy mixture. Add the flour and the
melted butter, stirring all the time with a spatula.
Then place small heaps of the mixture on the
sheet, just over 1 inch apart.
Flatten the heaps with the blade of a knife and
sprinkle with the almonds.
Put in the oven for about 8 minutes.
Roll up the squares while still warm, as soon as
they come out of the oven, by wrapping them
round a mini rolling pin (or wooden spoon
handle).

Cats' tongues (Langues de chat)

Serves 4
Preparation time: 20 minutes
Cooking time: 6 minutes

1 baking sheet

½ stick butter (at room temperature), cubed, +
¼ stick for greasing the baking sheet
½ cup confectioners' sugar
1 egg white
½ cup all-purpose flour

Preheat the oven to 350° F.
Grease the baking sheet with butter.
Cream together the butter and sugar to an oily consistency.
Whisk the egg white to form stiff peaks and fold them gently into the butter-sugar mixture, then pour in the flour in a stream, stirring all the time.
Line out the cats' tongues on the baking sheet leaving just over 1 inch between each one so that they do not touch during the cooking process.
You can do this with a piping bag and a quarter inch diameter nozzle, or shape them using two teaspoons.
Place in the oven for about 6 minutes. Keep a close eye on the cooking. They should be a pretty blond color and slightly brown at the edges.
Allow to cool before trying them.
You can easily keep them for several days in a cookie jar.

Chocolate cookies

Serves 4–6
Preparation time: 15 minutes
Cooking time: 10 minutes

1 baking sheet lined with nonstick baking paper

1 stick salted butter
7 oz best-quality dark chocolate
½ cup superfine sugar
1 cup all-purpose flour
1 teaspoon baking powder
1 egg
½ cup ground almonds

Preheat the oven to 400° F.
Slowly melt the butter in a small, heavy-based pan, then remove from the heat.
Grate the chocolate. Blend the melted butter and sugar to make a frothy mixture.
Mix the flour and baking powder in a bowl. Pour them into the butter-sugar mixture, together with the egg, almonds, and chocolate. Mix thoroughly.
Place the mixture in small rounds on the baking sheet, leaving a space between each one. Cook in the oven for 10 minutes.
Leave to cool before trying them.

New York brownies

Serves 4–6
Preparation time: 15 minutes
Cooking time: 25 minutes

1 square baking pan

7 oz best-quality dark chocolate
1 stick salted butter, at room temperature, cubed + ¼ stick for greasing the pan
¾ cup superfine sugar
3 eggs
½ cup all-purpose flour + 1 tablespoon for dusting the pan
1 cup hazelnuts or almonds, roughly chopped (optional)

Preheat the oven to 300° F.
Grease the pan with butter and lightly dust with flour.
Break the chocolate into pieces. Melt in a pan over boiling water or in a microwave oven.
In another bowl, work the butter and sugar together with a spatula to form a smooth paste. Add the eggs one by one, stirring all the time, then pour in the flour in a stream, still stirring.
Pour in the melted chocolate and the hazelnuts and mix well. Spread the mixture in the pan and cook in the oven for about 25 minutes.
Allow to cool before cutting into squares.

Muffins

Serves 4–6
Preparation time: 10 minutes
Cooking time: 20 minutes

12 muffin pans

1 stick salted butter + ¼ stick for greasing the pans
2½ cups all-purpose flour
½ teaspoon baking powder
1 teaspoon ground ginger
½ cup golden superfine sugar
1 cup chopped almonds
2 eggs
1 scant cup milk

Preheat the oven to 400° F.
Thoroughly grease the pans with butter.
Slowly melt the butter in a heavy-based saucepan.
Mix the flour, baking powder, and ginger in a bowl and then add the sugar and almonds.
Whisk the eggs and the milk in a large bowl. Add the melted butter and mix.
Fill three-quarters of each pan with the mixture.
Put in the oven for about 20 minutes.
Allow to cool for 5 minutes before removing the muffins from the pans.

VARIATION • You can replace the chopped almonds with golden raisins, chocolate drops, blackcurrants, or blueberries.

Buns, cookies, and other goodies

Chocolate truffles

Serves 4
Preparation time: 10 minutes
Cooking time: 5 minutes

4 oz best-quality dark chocolate
¼ cup superfine sugar
2 tablespoons milk
½ stick butter
1 fresh egg
4 tablespoons cocoa powder

Break the chocolate into small pieces and place them in a large, heavy-based saucepan with the sugar, milk, and butter.

Gently melt the mixture over a low heat, stirring all the time until it is completely smooth. Remove the pan from the heat.

Break the egg and separate the yolk from the white.

Pour the yolk into the chocolate cream and blend rapidly.

Leave the mixture to cool, then place in the refrigerator for about 1 hour while it sets. Then shape the truffles: pour some cocoa powder into a plate; take a ball of paste, and roll it quickly in the palm of your hand; then roll it in the cocoa powder.

Put the truffles in the refrigerator for at least 1 hour and serve while still cold.

TIP • If you like, you can flavour these truffles with alcohol: Grand Marnier, rum, or brandy for instance.

Eat them quickly (it will not be difficult!) as they are delicate and cannot be kept for long.

Christmas cookies

Makes about 2 lb 4 oz cookies
Preparation time: 20 minutes
Cooking time: 10–12 minutes per batch
Start the day before you want to cook them.

pastry cutters
1 baking sheet

2¼ sticks butter (at room temperature), cubed +
¼ stick for greasing the baking sheet
1 cup superfine sugar
3¼ cups all-purpose flour
1 cup ground almonds
2 whole eggs + 3 yolks
2 heaped teaspoons vanilla sugar (see page 12)
2 teaspoons ground cinnamon

Beat together the butter and sugar until the
mixture turns slightly pale. Add the flour and the
almonds, then the 2 whole eggs, beating all the
time. Pour in the vanilla sugar and the cinnamon
and stir.
Make the pastry into a ball, wrap it in plastic
wrap, and put it in the refrigerator for at least 3
hours. Ideally, you should prepare it the day
before and leave it to chill overnight.
Preheat the oven to 350° F.
Grease the baking sheet with the butter.
Take the pastry out of the refrigerator just before
you want to use it. Roll it out to a thickness of
about ⅛ inch, cut out the cookies with the pastry
cutters, and arrange them on the baking sheet.
Brush the tops with a little beaten egg yolk and
cook in the oven for 10–12 minutes.
Watch them carefully. When done, the cookies
should be a golden color.

Cinnamon and cider cakes

Serves 4–6
Preparation time: 15 minutes
Cooking time: 50 minutes

Individual round pans, tartlet pans, or a loaf pan

2 cups all-purpose flour
1 teaspoon baking powder
1 stick butter (at room temperature), cubed +
¼ stick for greasing the pan(s)
½ cup superfine sugar
2 eggs
1 teaspoon ground cinnamon
1 scant cup sweet cider

Preheat the oven to 350° F.
Grease the pans with butter.
Combine the flour and baking powder in a bowl.
Blend the butter and sugar in another bowl until
the mixture becomes slightly frothy and light
yellow in color, then add the eggs and half the
flour and cinnamon. Pour in the cider, a little at a
time, and the remainder of the flour in a stream.
Pour the mixture into the pans.
Put the tins in the oven for about 50 minutes.
Allow the cakes to cool for about 10 minutes
before removing them from the pans.

Breton cookies

Serves 6
Preparation time: 15 minutes
Cooking time: 25 minutes

This is a variation of the Galette Saint-Pierre (see
page 32). Use the same quantities and the same
proportions. Divide your mixture into as many
small pans as you like. They are really delicious
served with bergamot tea or strong coffee.

Monks' tartlets with dark chocolate

Makes 6 tartlets
Preparation time: 15 minutes
Cooking time: 20 minutes

6 tartlet pans 4 inches in diameter

¼ stick butter for greasing the pans
12 oz shortcrust pastry
4 oz best-quality dark chocolate
¾ cup ground almonds
½ cup golden raisins
½ cup pine nuts

Preheat the oven to 350° F.
Grease the pans with butter.
Roll out the shortcrust pastry and cut out 6 rounds
each approximately 6 inches in diameter.
Place one round of pastry in each pan, pressing
lightly into place with your fingers. Prick the bases
with a fork.
Break the chocolate into small pieces. Sprinkle the
ground almonds, the golden raisins, the pine
nuts, and the pieces of chocolate on the tart
bases.
Now cut out 6 more rounds of pastry
approximately 4 inches in diameter. Place them
over the contents of the tartlets, making sure that
the edges are sealed.
Put in the oven for about 20 minutes.
Remove the tartlets from the pans immediately
and leave to cool. They are delicious eaten warm.

Traditional Norfolk cakes

Serves 4–6
Preparation time: 10 minutes
Cooking time: 50 minutes

individual round pans, tartlet pans, or a loaf pan

2 cups all-purpose flour
1 teaspoon baking powder
1 stick salted butter, at room temperature,
cubed + ¼ stick for greasing the pan(s)
½ cup superfine sugar
2 cups golden raisins
1 tablespoon cider vinegar
½ cup milk

Preheat the oven to 350° F.
Grease the pans with butter.
Blend the flour and baking powder in a large
bowl. Add the butter and rub in with the
fingertips until it reaches a sandy consistency. Add
the sugar and the golden raisins. Pour in the cider
vinegar and then the milk. Mix well.
Pour the mixture into the pans.
Cook in the oven for about 50 minutes
Check to see if they are done by piercing one of
the cakes with the blade of a knife. It should
come out clean. Leave to cool before taking the
cakes out of the pans.

Flutes

Makes 24 cakes
Preparation time: 15 minutes
Cooking time: 1¼ hours
Prepare the day before you want to eat them.

24 flute or muffin pans

¼ stick butter for greasing the pans
1 whole egg + 4 yolks
4½ cups milk
2¼ cups superfine sugar
3 capfuls rum
5 drops vanilla extract
2 cups all-purpose flour

Blend the whole egg, yolks, milk, sugar, rum, and vanilla extract in a large bowl.
Put the flour in a basin; make a well in the flour, and add the mixture; mix well together, cover with plastic wrap and leave for 24 hours in the refrigerator.
Heat the oven to 300° F.
Grease the pans with butter.
Fill the pans two-thirds full with the mixture.
Cook for 1¼ hours. Remove the flutes from the pans and serve warm or cold.

Apple doughnuts

Serves 4–6
Preparation time: 20 minutes
Cooking time: 5 minutes

1 deep fryer

2 eggs
2 cups all-purpose flour
1 scant cup milk
¼ cup beer
¼ cup superfine sugar
2 pinches of salt
4 apples
oil for frying
confectioners' sugar

Break the eggs, separating the whites from the yolks.
Sift the flour, make a well, and gradually beat in the milk a little at a time, together with the beer, the 2 egg yolks, the sugar, and 1 pinch of salt.
When the mixture is smooth, put it in the refrigerator and leave it for at least 30 minutes.
Peel the apples, remove the cores and the seeds, and cut into rounds about ¼ inch thick.
Add the other pinch of salt to the egg whites and, using a whisk, beat until they form stiff peaks; then gently fold in the mixture from the refrigerator.
Heat the oil in the deep fryer.
Dip each apple round into the batter and then immediately into the hot oil. When the doughnuts have turned golden all over use a slotted spoon to lift them out of the oil.
Drain the doughnuts on kitchen towel. Dust them with confectioners' sugar just before serving.

Crunchy cookies

Serves 4–6
Preparation time: 15 minutes
Cooking time: 8 minutes

different shaped pastry cutters
1 baking sheet

1½ cups all-purpose flour
1 pinch of baking powder
1 stick salted butter (at room temperature), cubed + ¼ stick for greasing the baking sheet
¼ cup superfine sugar
1 egg
1 teaspoon vanilla extract
1 pinch of salt

Sift the flour and baking powder into a large bowl.
Tip the contents out onto your work surface and make a well in the flour. Fill the hollow with the butter and sugar and rub together with your fingertips, until the mixture resembles fine breadcrumbs.
Make another well and pour in the egg and vanilla extract. Add the salt and mix well.
Roll the pastry into a ball, wrap it in plastic wrap, and put it in the refrigerator for 2 hours.
Preheat the oven to 350° F.
Grease the baking sheet.
Roll out the pastry on a floured surface.
Cut out the cookies with pastry cutters and put them on the baking sheet.
Cook them in the oven for 6 to 8 minutes. The little cookies should take on a golden hue. Watch them carefully.
Then take them out of the oven and leave to cool.
They will keep for a few days in a cookie jar.

Palmiers

Serves 4–6
Preparation time: 10 minutes
Cooking time: 10 minutes

1 baking sheet lined with nonstick baking paper
1 cake rack

1 roll of puff pastry
½ cup superfine sugar

Preheat the oven to 350° F.
Roll out the pastry and dust with sugar, then roll each edge towards the middle. Place in the freezer for 5 minutes. Then cut it into thin strips and place them on the baking sheet.
Cook for about 10 minutes, taking care not to let them burn.
Leave to cool on a cake rack.

Almond dainties

Serves 4–6
Preparation time: 20 minutes
Cooking time: 12 minutes

1 bun sheet

½ stick salted butter + ¼ stick for greasing the cups
½ cup superfine sugar
1 cup ground almonds
2 eggs
1 tablespoon all-purpose flour

Preheat the oven to 375° F.
Grease the cups with butter.
Slowly melt the butter in a small heavy-based saucepan.
Mix the sugar and ground almonds in a bowl then gradually add the eggs.
Pour in the melted butter and mix well.
Finally, add the flour, stirring all the time.
Fill the cups with the mixture and cook in the oven for about 12 minutes.

Some exotic variations
With ginger

For a slightly more spicy flavour, add 2 tablespoons of chopped preserved ginger to your mixture.

With green tea

Add 2 teaspoons of powdered green tea to the ground almonds. (Green tea powder is available at shops selling Chinese specialties.)

Almond and orange cake

Serves 6
Preparation time: 10 minutes
Cooking time: 40 minutes

1 loaf pan, or a number of small pans

¼ stick butter for greasing the pan(s)
½ cup all-purpose flour
1 teaspoon baking powder
6 eggs
½ cup superfine sugar
1 pinch of salt
2 cups ground almonds
grated rind of 1 unwaxed orange
juice of 2 oranges

Preheat the oven to 350° F.
Grease the pan(s) with butter.
Mix together the flour and baking powder.
Break the eggs and separate the whites from the yolks.
Whisk the yolks and sugar together until the mixture turns slightly pale. Combine with the flour and baking powder.
Add the pinch of salt to the egg whites and whisk into firm peaks with an electric beater (or hand whisk).
Then add the ground almonds to the first mixture, pour in the orange rind and juice, and fold in the beaten egg whites a little at a time, using sweeping movements so as not to break down the egg whites. Fill the pan(s) with this mixture and put in the oven for 40 minutes.
Decorate the cake(s) when cool with a little confectioners' sugar, or coat with vanilla frosting.

Almond dainties with green tea

Almond antlers

Serves 6–8
Preparation time: 30 minutes
Cooking time: 10–15 minutes

1 baking sheet
1 cake rack

4½ cups ground almonds
½ cup superfine sugar
2¼ sticks salted butter (at room temperature) +
¼ stick for greasing the baking sheet
1 tablespoon water
4½ cups all-purpose flour + 2 tablespoons for
dusting the baking sheet
1 pinch of salt
3 tablespoons orange flower water
confectioners' sugar

Almond pastry

Mix the ground almonds and sugar with
¼ stick butter. Add a tablespoon of water to make
a smooth paste. Knead it with your fingertips,
then leave for about 30 minutes.

Cookie mixture

Melt the rest of the butter in a small, heavy-based
saucepan. Then mix in a large bowl with the flour,
add the salt, and stir well. The mixture should be
fairly firm.

Making the cookies

Preheat the oven to 300° F.
Grease the baking sheet and dust with flour.
Sprinkle flour on your work surface and roll out
the pastry thinly. Cut out small rectangles using a
pastry wheel.
Roll the almond paste into little sausage shapes
and place in the middle of each pastry rectangle.
Roll up the pastry into the shape of a horn.
Place the crescent shapes on the baking sheet.
Cook in the oven for about 10 minutes.
Keep an eye on the cooking as they must not be
allowed to brown.
Sprinkle lightly with orange flower water, then roll
them gently in the confectioners' sugar. Put them
on a cake rack and leave to cool.

Apple and cinnamon turnovers

Serves 4–6
Preparation time: 15 minutes
Cooking time: 40 minutes

1 baking sheet lined with nonstick baking paper

1 lb 2 oz apples
2 tablespoons water
4 tablespoons superfine sugar
½ teaspoon ground cinnamon
14 oz puff pastry
1 egg yolk

Peel and quarter the apples, removing the cores and seeds. Put them in a pan with 2 tablespoons of water and the sugar.
Bring to the boil, then turn down the heat. Leave to cook slowly for about 15 minutes. Dust with the ground cinnamon.
Preheat the oven to 350° F.
Roll out the pastry and cut out rounds about 4½ inches in diameter.
Spread the apple compote over half of each round, leaving a space round the edge. Moisten the edges slightly and fold over the pastry to make the turnover. Glaze with a little beaten egg yolk and put in the oven. Cook for about 20–25 minutes.
Serve warm or cold.
You can decorate your turnovers with raw apple if you like.

Marvels

These little marvels used to be served on Shrove Tuesday in some countries, but of course you can make them all the year round … and preferably with the help of children (they love making them!).

Preparation time: 15 minutes
Cooking time: 4 minutes

1 deep fryer

4½ cups all-purpose flour
2 teaspoons baking powder
½ cup superfine sugar
1 stick salted butter (at room temperature), cubed
4 eggs
2 tablespoons rum
confectioners' sugar

Mix the flour and baking powder then make a well. Put the sugar, cubed butter, eggs, and rum into the hollow.
Mix with the fingertips then roll the dough into a ball and wrap in plastic wrap. Put in the refrigerator for about 30 minutes.
Divide the dough into 3 or 4 balls then roll out each one on a lightly floured surface.
Cut out small rectangles of dough about 1½ inches wide. Make a slit in the middle and fold back a flap of dough to resemble a bow.
Heat the oil in a fryer. Drop in a bit of pastry—if it rises to the surface, the oil is at the right temperature.
Cook the marvels by plunging them into the cooking oil. Watch them carefully, as the marvels need to be just right: golden, but not burnt.
Drain on kitchen towel. Dust with confectioners' sugar and serve immediately.
They can also be kept for several days in a cookie jar.

Apple and cinnamon turnovers

Choux pastry puffs

The great thing about choux pastry is that everyone is impressed by it—even the cook! Yet nothing could be easier. Have a go!

Serves 4
Preparation time: 15 minutes
Cooking time: 25 minutes

1 baking sheet lined with nonstick baking paper

½ stick butter
1 scant cup water
¾ cup all-purpose flour
2 eggs
1 pinch of salt
2 tablespoons candy sugar (as illustrated)

Preheat the over to 300–350° F.
Put the butter and water in a small, heavy-based saucepan to heat. As soon as the first bubbles form, remove the pan from the heat.
Pour in the flour all at once and mix with a spoon, until the mixture turns into a rubbery ball that detaches easily from the sides of the pan.
Add the eggs one at a time, stirring constantly, then add the salt. Your mixture should have a smooth but firm consistency.
Use 2 spoons to form small balls and arrange them on the baking sheet.
Warning! Leave a generous space between the puffs as they rise during cooking.
Put in the oven for about 15 minutes.
Remove from the oven and dust with candy sugar.

Milk rolls

Serves 4–6
Preparation time: 25 minutes
Cooking time: 12 minutes

1 baking sheet lined with nonstick baking paper

½ oz dried yeast
4 tablespoons + 4 tablespoons milk
2 cups all-purpose flour
2 tablespoons superfine sugar
1 pinch of salt
1 whole egg + 1 yolk
½ stick salted butter (at room temperature), cubed

Dissolve the yeast in 4 tablespoons warm milk (or follow instructions on the packet).
Pour the flour, sugar, salt, the milk-yeast mixture, and the whole egg into the bowl of your food processor. Blend, then pour in the rest of the milk and blend some more.
Knead the dough a little until smooth. Add the cubed butter and knead again.
Then form the dough into a ball and put it in a warm place covered with a dish towel. Leave for about 45 minutes, by which time it should have doubled in volume.
Preheat the oven to 410° F.
Glaze the buns with a little beaten egg yolk and put in the oven. Lower the temperature to 350° F and cook for about 12 minutes. Be vigilant during the cooking process. The rolls will be slightly brown underneath when done.
Using the same dough recipe, you can make different shapes: plaits, coils, etc.

Choux pastry puffs

Currant buns

It is very satisfying to make your own bread. Depending on your mood, you can use chopped hazelnuts or walnuts instead of currants.

Serves 4–6
Preparation time: 20 minutes
Cooking time: 15 minutes

1 baking sheet lined with nonstick baking paper

1 sachet dried yeast
½ cup water
2½ cups all-purpose flour
1 cup wholewheat flour
1 tablespoon salted butter (at room temperature), cubed
1 tablespoon superfine sugar
1 scant tablespoon salt
2 cups currants or golden raisins

Dissolve the yeast in 4 tablespoons warm water (or follow directions on the packet).
Put the white flour, wholewheat flour, butter, sugar, salt, and yeast in a bowl.
Using a food processor with a dough attachment if available, mix on a slow speed then pour in the remaining water, a little at a time. (Alternatively you can mix by hand using a spoon.)
Knead by hand for a few seconds until the dough forms a ball.
Put the dough in a warm place and cover with a dish towel. Leave it until it doubles in volume.
Add the currants or golden raisins, knead again for a few seconds, then form dough into small balls and arrange them on the baking sheet.
Cover with a dish towel and leave to rise again for about 45 minutes.
Preheat the oven to 410° F.
Brush the buns with a little water and bake them for about 15 minutes.
Check to see if they are done by tapping the bases of the buns. If they sound hollow, they are cooked!

Delicious easy-to-make cakes

Delicious easy-to-make cakes

Yogurt cake with jelly

Yogurt cake

Without doubt, yogurt cake has many outstanding advantages: it is very easy to make and always turns out well; it is also infinitely versatile. Use the empty yogurt container to measure the ingredients. Here are a few examples. You can also invent your own.

Serves 4–6
Preparation time: 15 minutes
Cooking time: 35 minutes

1 deep cake pan in diameter

1 tablespoon butter for greasing the pan
1 small container of natural yogurt
2 containers of sugar
3 eggs
3 containers of all-purpose flour
2 teaspoons baking powder
1 container of cooking oil

Preheat the oven to 350° F.
Grease the pan with butter.
Pour the yogurt into a basin, then rinse out the container and use it to measure the other ingredients.
Combine the yogurt, sugar and eggs; mix until frothy. Add the flour and baking powder; mix again, then add the oil.
Put the mixture into the pan. Cook for about 35 minutes. Remove from the pan while still warm.

Simple variations

Replace the container of oil with the same weight in butter.
Replace the container of oil with heavy cream (the cake will be paler).
Substitute 1 container of ground almonds for 1 container of flour.

Pineapple upside-down cake

yogurt cake mixture (see above)
1 small can of pineapple slices in syrup
1 vanilla bean
1 tablespoon rum
rind of 1 lemon

For the caramel:
1½ tablespoons salted butter
3 tablespoons demerara or soft brown sugar
1 tablespoon pineapple syrup

First caramelize the pineapple: chop up 3 slices of the pineapple and leave to cook in a saucepan with the vanilla bean for about 10 minutes over a low heat.
Grease the pan well and arrange slices of pineapple over the base. Caramelize the butter, sugar, and 1 tablespoon of pineapple juice in a saucepan: heat slowly while the sugar dissolves, then turn up the heat and watch carefully. When

the mixture has caramelized slightly, pour it over the pineapple in the base of the pan.
Prepare the yogurt cake mixture following the basic recipe and then add the rum, the lemon rind, and the chopped, cooked pineapple.
Cover the pineapple slices with the mixture and cook in the oven for about 40 minutes at 350° F. When cooked, take the cake out of the oven and leave to stand for about 15 minutes before removing from the pan.

Lemon cake

yogurt cake mixture (see above)
juice of 2 lemons
½ container of confectioners' sugar
rind of 1 lemon

Follow the basic recipe, adding the lemon rind at the end. Bake in the oven for about 40 minutes at 350° F.
When the cake is cooked, take it out of the oven and allow to cool before removing it from the pan.
Make the lemon glaze by mixing the lemon juice and sugar. Brush over the cake, adding a little lemon peel for decoration.

Rum baba cake

yogurt cake mixture made with ground almonds (see under 'Simple variations' above)
1½ cups rum
1½ cups water
3 tablespoons demerara sugar

Follow the basic recipe. Cook for about 350° F.
While the cake is cooking, boil the rum, water, and sugar together over a low heat to make syrup. Remove the cake from the oven when cooked and douse with the syrup repeatedly until the baba is completely saturated. Leave to cool. Gently remove from the pan.

VARIATION • You can replace the rum with cherry juice mixed with kirsch, but leave out the sugar. Arrange about 20 cherries in the pan before pouring in the cake mixture.

Apple cake

yogurt cake mixture made with heavy cream (see under 'Simple variations' above)
3 or 4 good quality apples, slightly acidic, chopped
rind of 1 lemon

Follow the basic recipe. At the end, add the chopped apples and the lemon rind.
Put in the oven for 40 minutes at 350° F.
When the cake is cooked, take it out of the oven and wait about 15 minutes before removing it from the pan.

Savoy sponge cake

Serves 4–6
Preparation time: 15 minutes
Cooking time: 35 minutes

1 deep cake pan about 9 inches in diameter

1½ tablespoons butter for greasing the pan
1½ tablespoons all-purpose flour for dusting the pan
4 eggs
½ cup superfine sugar
½ cup cornstarch
1 pinch of salt

Preheat the oven to 300° F.
Thoroughly grease the pan with butter and dust with flour.
Separate the egg yolks from the whites. Using an electric mixer if you wish, whisk together the yolks and sugar until frothy. Gradually add the cornstarch. Mix well.
Add the salt to the egg whites and beat until stiff white peaks are formed, then gently fold into the yolks-sugar mixture using a spatula so as not to deflate the egg whites. The mixture should be quite smooth.
Pour the mixture into the pan.
Put in the oven and bake for about 35 minutes.

Genoese sponge cake

You can also use this recipe to make a chocolate Genoese sponge. All you do is replace 4 tablespoons of flour with 4 tablespoons cocoa powder.

Serves 4–6
Preparation time: 10 minutes
Cooking time: 25 minutes

1 deep cake pan about 9 inches in diameter
1 cake rack

1½ tablespoons butter for greasing the pan
½ cup superfine sugar
4 eggs
1 cup all-purpose flour + 1½ tablespoons for dusting the pan

Preheat the oven to 300° F.
Grease the pan and dust lightly with flour.
Put the sugar and eggs in a large bowl.
Heat a large saucepan of water. When it reaches simmering point, place the bowl in the water. Whisk until the mixture thickens, then remove the bowl from the water and continue to beat for a few more seconds.
Add the flour a little at a time, still mixing and lifting the mixture with a spatula.
Spread the mixture in the pan. Smooth the surface with a spatula.
Cook for about 25 minutes. The cake is ready when it is a lovely golden color.
As soon as it is done, remove the sponge from the pan and leave to cool on a cake rack.

Chocolate sandwich cake

Serves 4–6
Preparation time: 30 minutes
Cooking time: 40 minutes

1 Savoy sponge cake (see page 64)
7 oz best-quality dark chocolate
2 tablespoons heavy cream
4 eggs

Soften the chocolate in boiling water for 20 minutes then pour off the hot water, leaving the chocolate. Immediately add the cream and mix well.
Separate the egg whites from the yolks.
Fold the yolks into chocolate one at a time. Beat the egg whites on a medium speed (or use a hand whisk) to form stiff peaks, adding a pinch of sugar half way through; then increase the speed. Fold the beaten egg whites into the chocolate mixture. Refrigerate for a few hours.
Meanwhile, make a Savoy sponge cake in a 9 inch diameter pan. When cooked, remove immediately from the pan. Leave to cool, then cut in two horizontally.
Fill with the chocolate cream. Replace the top and keep in a cool place.

Mocha sandwich cake

Serves 4–6
Preparation time: 30 minutes
Cooking time: 40 minutes

1 Savoy sponge cake (see page 64)
butter cream (see page 20)
coffee extract

Make a Savoy sponge cake. Take it out of the pan as soon as it is done and leave to cool.
Cut it in two horizontally.
Fill with butter cream mixed with coffee extract. Replace the top. Coat the whole cake in butter cream and keep in a cool place.

Chestnut sandwich cake

Serves 4–6
Preparation time: 30 minutes
Cooking time: 40 minutes

1 Savoy sponge cake (see page 64)
3 large meringues
8 oz chestnut spread

If you are unable to buy ready-made chestnut spread, you can make your own (see page 152).
Crumble the meringues.
Whip the chestnut spread and combine with the meringues.
Cut the sponge cake in half and spread one half with the chestnut-meringue mixture. Replace the top.
Heat a little chestnut spread with some water to glaze the cake.

Strawberry sandwich cake

Serves 4–6
Preparation time: 30 minutes
Cooking time: 40 minutes

1 Genoese sponge cake (see page 66)
3 egg whites
1 cup superfine sugar
1¾ sticks butter
kirsch
8 oz raspberry jello
1 lb 2 oz strawberries

Make a Genoese sponge cake in a deep cake pan, 9 inches in diameter. As soon as it is done, remove the cake from the pan and leave to cool.
Whisk the egg whites with the sugar in a bowl over a pan of hot water, until the mixture resembles a shiny mousse.
Cream the butter and flavor it with a little kirsch. Gently fold the beaten egg whites into the butter cream.
Depending on the height of the sponge cake, slice it in 2 or 3 horizontally. Spread the bottom section with a layer of raspberry jello, then a thicker layer of butter cream.
Cut the strawberries in half and arrange them on top of the butter cream. Cover with the second layer of cake. Spread with raspberry jello, cream, and fruit as before. Cover with the top layer of cake.
To decorate, coat the cake with the remaining butter cream and strawberries.

Lemon curd sandwich cake

Serves 4–6
Preparation time: 30 minutes
Cooking time: 40 minutes
Serves 4–6

1 Savoy sponge cake (see page 64)
3 egg whites
½ cup sugar
4 oz lemon curd
2 tablespoons poppy seeds
confectioners' sugar
juice of 1 lemon

Make a Savoy sponge cake; remove it from the pan as soon as it is cooked.
Whisk the egg whites with the sugar over a bowl of hot water, until the mixture resembles a shiny mousse.
Beat the lemon curd with a spatula and gently fold it into the beaten egg whites together with 1 tablespoonful of poppy seeds.
Slice the sponge cake in two horizontally. Spread the base with the lemon mousse. Cover with the top layer.
Dilute a little confectioners' sugar in some lemon juice. Pour it over the cake and sprinkle with the remaining poppy seeds.

Pound cake

This cake is infinitely variable depending on your taste and the contents of your cupboard! You simply weigh 3 eggs (in their shells), then weigh out the same amount of flour, sugar, and butter.

Serves 4
Preparation time: 15 minutes
Cooking time: 35–40 minutes

1 deep cake pan, 9 inches in diameter

3 medium eggs weighing about 2 oz each + 1 yolk
salted butter, cubed (at room temperature): the same weight as the eggs + 1 knob of butter
sugar: the same weight as the 3 eggs
all-purpose flour: the same weight as the eggs
1 teaspoon baking powder

Preheat the oven to 300° F.
Thoroughly grease the pan with the knob of butter.
Put the butter in a large basin and cream it with a spatula, then add the sugar and beat until the mixture turns pale and creamy. Add the eggs and yolk and mix well.
Quickly sift the flour and baking powder and fold into the contents of the basin.
The mixture should be completely smooth.
Pour into the cake pan and put in the oven. Leave to cook for about 40 minutes.
You can tell if it is done by piercing the center of the cake with a knife: the blade should come out clean.
Allow the cake to cool before taking it out of the pan.

Orange pound cake

Serves 4
Preparation time: 15 minutes
Cooking time: 35–40 minutes

1 deep cake pan, 9 inches in diameter

3 medium eggs weighing about 2 oz each + 1 yolk
salted butter, cubed (at room temperature): the same weight as the 3 eggs + 1 knob of butter
sugar: the same weight as the eggs
all-purpose flour: the same weight as the eggs
1 teaspoon baking powder
2 teaspoons grated orange rind

Preheat the oven to 300° F.
Thoroughly grease the pan with the knob of butter.
Put the rest of the butter in a large basin and cream it with a spatula, then add the sugar and beat until the mixture turns pale and creamy. Add the eggs and yolk and mix well.
Quickly sift the flour and baking powder into a large bowl and pour them into the mixture.
Add the orange rind and mix again. The mixture should be completely smooth.
Pour it into the pan and put in the oven to cook for about 40 minutes.
You can tell if it is done by piercing the center of the cake with a knife: the blade should come out clean.
Allow the cake to cool before taking it out of the pan.

Apple pound cake

Serves 4
Preparation time: 15 minutes
Cooking time: 35–40 minutes

1 deep cake pan, 9 inches in diameter

2 good quality apples
juice of 1 lemon
3 medium eggs weighing about 2 oz each + 1 yolk
salted butter, cubed (at room temperature): the same weight as the 3 eggs + 1 knob of butter for greasing the pan
sugar: the same weight as the eggs
all-purpose flour: the same weight as the eggs
1 teaspoon baking powder

Preheat the oven to 300° F.
Thoroughly grease the pan with the knob of butter.
Peel and quarter the apples, and remove the cores and seeds. Roughly chop the quarters and sprinkle them with the lemon juice.
Put the butter in a large basin and cream it with a spatula, then pour in the sugar and beat until the mixture becomes pale and creamy. Add the eggs and yolk and mix well.
Quickly sift and mix the flour and baking powder in a large bowl and pour them into the basin. The mixture should be completely smooth. Add the chopped apple and mix.
Pour the mixture into the pan and put in the oven to cook for about 40 minutes. You can tell if it is done by piercing the center of the cake with a knife: the blade should come out clean.
Allow the cake to cool before taking it out of the pan.

Spice cake

Serves 6
Preparation time: 15 minutes
Cooking time: 50 minutes

1 loaf pan

1½ tablespoons butter for greasing the pan
½ cup milk
1½ cups good quality runny honey
2 cups whole-wheat flour
2 teaspoons baking powder
½ cup ground almonds
1 tablespoon ground mixed spices (cinnamon,
cloves, ginger, and aniseed)
3 tablespoons chopped candied orange peel
1 egg

Preheat the oven to 325° F.
Grease the pan with the butter.
Gently heat the milk and honey together—
remove from heat when bubbles start to form.
Sift the flour and baking powder together into a
bowl, then mix in the ground almonds, spices,
and chopped candied orange peel. Make a well in
the center, then pour in the milk-honey mixture,
stirring all the time with a spoon. Finish by stirring
in the egg.
Pour the mixture into the pan and cook in the
oven for about 50 minutes.

Chocolate chip cake

Serves 4–6
Preparation time: 10 minutes
Cooking time: 40 minutes

1 square cake pan or a loaf pan

1 cup all-purpose flour
1 teaspoon baking powder
3 oz best-quality dark chocolate
1 stick salted butter (at room temperature),
cubed + 1½ tablespoons for greasing the pan
1 cup confectioners' sugar
2 tablespoons ground almonds
1 tablespoon cocoa powder
2 eggs
½ teaspoon vanilla extract
5 tablespoons chocolate chips

Preheat the oven to 410° F.
Thoroughly grease the pan. Combine the flour
and baking powder. Grate the dark chocolate.
Beat the butter and confectioners' sugar with a
wooden spoon until the mixture turns smooth
and creamy. Gradually add the ground almonds,
the flour-baking powder mixture, the cocoa
powder, the grated chocolate, and the eggs,
stirring all the time.
Add the vanilla extract and the chocolate chips.
Transfer the mixture to the pan, lower the
temperature of the oven to 350° F, and cook for
about 40 minutes.
Serve warm or cold.
If you like, you can sprinkle the cake with two or
three tablespoons of rum when you take it out of
the oven.

Easy bitter chocolate cake

Serves 4–6
Preparation time: 20 minutes
Cooking time: 30 minutes

1 round or square tart pan

7 oz best-quality dark chocolate
4 eggs
1 pinch of salt
1¼ sticks salted butter, cubed (at room
temperature) + 1½ tablespoons for greasing the
pan
½ cup sugar
½ cup all-purpose flour

Preheat the oven to 350° F.
Thoroughly grease the pan with the butter.
Half fill a saucepan with water and bring to the
boil. Break the chocolate into pieces and put it to
melt in a bowl resting over the pan (but not
touching the water).
Break the eggs, separating the whites from the
yolks. Beat the whites to form soft peaks, adding
a pinch of salt.
Roughly combine the butter and sugar; add the
melted chocolate, stirring all the time, then mix in
the yolks, still stirring. Add the flour and finally
the beaten egg whites in three stages. Mix gently
until smooth.
Put the mixture into the pan, lower the oven
temperature to 300° F, and cook the cake for
about 30 minutes.
Allow to cool slightly before removing it from the
pan—it will be harder to take out later on.

VARIATION • For a change, you can always add
some slivered almonds or small pieces of candied
(crystallized) orange.

Easy bitter chocolate cake

Delicious easy-to-make cakes

Walnut cake

Serves 4–6
Preparation time: 15 minutes
Cooking time: 30 minutes

1 deep cake pan, about 9 inches in diameter

4 eggs
½ cup golden superfine sugar
6 tablespoons salted butter + 1½ tablespoons for greasing the pan
½ cup all-purpose flour + 1½ tablespoons for dusting the pan
1½ cups crushed walnut kernels
1 pinch of salt

Preheat the oven to 410° F.
Grease the pan with the butter and dust lightly with flour. Remove excess flour by tapping the upturned pan.
Break the eggs, separating the whites from the yolks. Mix the yolks with the sugar using a whisk. Gently melt the butter in a small, heavy-based saucepan, then pour it into the egg-sugar mixture. Mix well, then gradually add the flour and nut kernels.
Add the pinch of salt to the egg whites and beat them into soft peaks. Fold them into the mixture a little at a time, using a wooden spoon so they do not break down.
Spread the mixture in the pan and cook for about 30 minutes. Allow to cool before removing it from the pan.

VARIATION • You can use the same recipe to make a hazelnut cake simply by substituting hazelnuts for the walnuts.

Banana and rum cake

Serves 4–6
Preparation time: 20 minutes
Cooking time: 40 minutes

1 loaf pan

2 ripe bananas
juice of 1 lemon
1½ tablespoons rum
1 stick salted butter (at room temperature), cubed + 1½ tablespoons for greasing the pan
½ cup superfine sugar
2 eggs
4 oz best-quality dark chocolate
2 cups all-purpose flour + 1½ tablespoons for dusting the pan
2 teaspoons baking powder
1 pinch of salt
1 teaspoon vanilla extract

Preheat the oven to 350° F.
Thoroughly grease the pan and dust with flour. Peel the bananas and mash them with a fork. Pour the lemon juice and rum over the purée. Beat the butter and sugar together in a large bowl. As soon as the mixture turns pale, add the eggs one at a time while continuing to beat. Grate the chocolate.
In another bowl, mix the flour and baking powder. Add the pinch of salt then pour into the bowl containing the butter and sugar mixture. Mix well, then add the banana purée and vanilla extract.
Put the mixture into the loaf pan and cook in the oven for about 40 minutes.
For a stronger flavor, sprinkle the cake with three or four tablespoons of rum when you take it out of the oven.

Walnut cake

Banana and walnut cake

Serves 4–6
Preparation time: 15 minutes
Cooking time: 50 minutes

1 loaf pan

3 ripe bananas
2 cups all-purpose flour
1 teaspoon baking powder
1 stick salted butter, cubed (at room temperature) + 1½ tablespoons for greasing the pan
½ cup superfine sugar
2 eggs
1 teaspoon vanilla extract
½ cup chopped walnuts

Preheat the oven to 350° F.
Grease the pan with the butter.
Peel the bananas and mash them with a fork.
Mix the flour and baking powder in a bowl.
Mix the bananas, butter, sugar, flour, eggs, and vanilla extract in the bowl of your electric mixer, then add the chopped walnuts. Spread the mixture in the pan and cook for about 50 minutes in the oven.
Allow to cool for about 10 minutes before taking the cake out of the pan.
This cake tastes even better the next day.

Hazelnut and honey cake

Serves 4–6
Preparation time: 10 minutes
Cooking time: 25 minutes

1 deep cake pan, 9 inches in diameter, or an assortment of small pans

3 eggs
1 pinch of salt
6 tablespoons superfine sugar
6 tablespoons all-purpose flour
½ cup chopped or ground hazelnuts
¾ stick butter + 1½ tablespoons for greasing the pan
4 tablespoons honey

Preheat the oven to 350° F.
Grease the pan(s) with the butter.
Break the eggs, separating the whites from the yolks.
Add the pinch of salt to the egg whites and, using a whisk, beat them until they form stiff peaks.
In a large bowl, mix the sugar, flour, egg yolks, and chopped hazelnuts.
Melt the butter and honey in a heavy-based saucepan, then pour this mixture into the large bowl, stirring all the time.
Gently fold in the egg whites using a wooden spatula to avoid breaking down the whites.
Pour the mixture into the pan(s) and cook in the oven for about 25 minutes.
Allow the cake to cool before taking it out of the pan(s).

Hazelnut and honey cake

Carrot and raisin cake

Serves 4–6
Preparation time: 15 minutes
Cooking time: 45 minutes

1 loaf pan or deep cake pan

½ cup golden raisins
3 tablespoons rum
4 eggs
1 stick salted butter, cubed (at room temperature) + 1½ tablespoons for greasing the pan
1½ cups golden superfine sugar
3 cups all-purpose flour
2 teaspoons baking powder
14 oz carrots, finely grated
1 teaspoon ground cinnamon
1 teaspoon ground ginger
¼ teaspoon grated nutmeg

Preheat the oven to 300° F.
Thoroughly grease the pan with the butter.
Soak the golden raisins in a bowl with the rum.
Whisk the eggs at high speed in a large bowl, then add the butter and sugar and blend until the mixture turns creamy.
Mix the flour and the baking powder in another bowl and pour into the butter-eggs-sugar mixture in a stream. Add the carrots, golden raisins soaked in rum, cinnamon, ginger, and nutmeg and mix well.
Pour into the pan and cook in the oven for about 45 minutes.
Allow to cool before taking the cake out of the pan.
You can enjoy this cake warm or cold. It is especially good the next day.

You can substitute ½ cup pine kernels or ¾ cup ground almonds for the golden raisins if you like.

Almond and carrot cake

Serves 4–6
Preparation time: 20 minutes
Cooking time: 40 minutes

1 loaf pan

1½ tablespoons butter for greasing the pan
5 eggs
1 cup all-purpose flour + 1½ tablespoons for dusting the pan
6 oz carrots, grated
2 cups ground almonds
grated rind of 2 unwaxed oranges
½ cup golden superfine sugar
1 pinch of salt

Preheat the oven to 410° F.
Thoroughly grease the pan and dust with flour.
Break the eggs, separating the yolks from the whites.
Mix together the flour, grated carrot, ground almonds, and grated orange rind in a large bowl.
Whisk the egg yolks and sugar in another bowl, then combine them with the ingredients in the large bowl.
Add the pinch of salt to the egg whites and beat them using your electric mixer (or a hand whisk) until they form soft peaks. Gently fold them into the mixture in the large bowl.
Cook in the oven for about 40 minutes.
Allow the cake to cool before taking it out of the pan.
To serve, dust the cake with a little confectioners' sugar.
You can enhance the flavor of your cake by adding ½ teaspoon freshly milled cardamom seeds to the mixture before cooking.

Carrot and golden raisin cake

Lemon and almond cake

Serves 4–6
Preparation time: 20 minutes
Cooking time: 40 minutes

1 loaf pan

1 scant cup superfine sugar
1¾ sticks salted butter (at room temperature),
cubed + 1½ tablespoons for greasing the pan
2 cups ground almonds
3 eggs
juice and rind of an unwaxed lemon
1 cup maize flour (or whole-wheat flour)
+ 1½ tablespoons for dusting the pan
1 teaspoon baking powder
1 pinch of salt

Preheat the oven to 350° F.
Thoroughly grease the pan and dust with flour.
Beat the sugar and butter together in a large
bowl. When the mixture turns pale, add the
ground almonds and then the eggs, one at a
time, and mix. Then add the lemon juice and rind.
In another bowl, mix the flour and baking
powder. Add the pinch of salt, then add to the
bowl containing the butter, sugar, almonds, eggs,
and lemon. Mix well.
Pour the mixture into the pan. Place the pan on a
baking sheet in the oven and cook for about 40
minutes.
Serve very fresh.

Chestnut and vanilla cake

Serves 4–6
Preparation time: 15 minutes
Cooking time: 30 minutes

1 round pan, or charlotte mold if you have one

3 eggs
1 pinch of salt
1 stick salted butter + 1½ tablespoons for greasing the pan
1 lb 2 oz pure chestnut purée
½ cup superfine sugar
2 teaspoons vanilla extract

Preheat the oven to 350° F.
Grease the pan with butter.
Break the eggs, separating the whites from the yolks.
Add the pinch of salt to the whites and, using an electric mixer (or a hand whisk), beat until stiff white peaks form.
Slowly melt the butter in a small, heavy-based saucepan.
In a large bowl, blend the chestnut purée, egg yolks, sugar, melted butter, and vanilla extract.
Gently fold in the whites of egg using a spatula, so they do not break down during the blending.
Pour the mixture into the pan and smooth the surface with the spatula.
Put in the oven and cook for about 30 minutes. Allow the cake to cool before taking it out of the pan.

TIP • Serve very fresh with custard or heavy cream.

Marbled cake

Serves 4–6
Preparation time: 15 minutes
Cooking time: 30 minutes

1 loaf pan
1 cake rack

1 stick salted butter (at room temperature), cubed + 1½ tablespoons for greasing the pan
½ cup superfine sugar
2 eggs
4 tablespoons milk
2 cups all-purpose flour + 1½ tablespoons for dusting the pan
1 teaspoon baking powder
1 pinch of salt
½ teaspoon vanilla sugar (see page 12)
1 tablespoon cocoa powder

Preheat the oven to 410° F.
Grease the pan with the butter and dust with flour.
Using an electric whisk, beat the butter and sugar together until the mixture turns pale and frothy.
Break the eggs, separating the whites from the yolks. Stir the yolks into the butter-sugar mixture, then add the milk, a little at a time, stirring as you pour.
Mix the flour and baking powder together in a large bowl, then stir them into the mixture.
Add the pinch of salt to the whites and beat them into stiff peaks with an electric whisk.
Divide the mixture into 2 bowls.
Pour the vanilla sugar into the first and the cocoa powder into the second. Then gently fold half the egg whites into the vanilla flavoured mixture, using a spatula to mix in the whites without breaking them down. Fold the rest into the chocolate mixture.
Spread a layer of the vanilla mixture in the base of the pan then cover it with a layer of the chocolate. Repeat until the mixtures are used up.
Put the cake in the oven for 10 minutes then lower the heat to 350° F and cook for another 20 minutes.
Remove the cake from the pan and allow to cool on a cake rack.

Marbled cake

Golden raisin and ginger cake

Serves 4–6
Preparation time: 20 minutes
Cooking time: 40 minutes

1 loaf pan

1½ cups golden raisins
1 tablespoon rum
1 stick salted butter (at room temperature),
cubed + 1½ tablespoons for greasing the pan
½ cup sugar
2 eggs
2 cups all-purpose flour + 1½ tablespoons for
dusting the pan
2 teaspoons baking powder
1 pinch of salt
1 tablespoon ground ginger

Put the golden raisins to soak in a bowl with the rum.
Preheat the oven to 350° F.
Thoroughly grease the pan and dust with flour.
Beat the butter and sugar together in a large bowl. When the mixture turns pale, gradually add the eggs, stirring all the time.
In another bowl, mix the flour with the baking powder.
Add the pinch of salt and ground ginger, then pour the mixture into the bowl containing the butter and sugar. Blend well and add the golden raisins.
Spread the mixture in the pan, place on a baking sheet, and cook in the oven for about 40 minutes.

VARIATION • You can substitute candied orange peel for the golden raisins.

Date and ginger cake

Serves 4–6
Preparation time: 10 minutes
Cooking time: 50 minutes

1 loaf pan

1 cup pitted dates
2 cups all-purpose flour
1 teaspoon baking powder
1½ sticks salted butter (at room temperature),
cubed + 1½ tablespoons for greasing the pan
10 tablespoons superfine sugar
2 eggs
1 teaspoon vanilla extract
1 scant cup milk
2 tablespoons chopped, preserved ginger

Preheat the oven to 350° F.
Grease the pan with the butter.
Chop the dates with a knife. Mix the flour and baking powder in a bowl.
In a large bowl, blend the butter and sugar, then add the flour in a stream. Blend in the eggs, chopped dates, vanilla extract, and the milk, stirring all the time. Finally, add the chopped preserved ginger.
Spread the mixture in the pan. Cook in the oven for about 50 minutes.
Allow to cool before taking the cake out of the pan.

Date and ginger cake

Fruit cake (with a difference)

Serves 4–6
Preparation time: 20 minutes
Cooking time: 45 minutes

1 loaf pan

¾ cup golden raisins
1 tablespoon rum
1 stick salted butter (at room temperature), cubed + 1½ tablespoons for greasing the pan
½ cup superfine sugar
2 eggs
2 cups all-purpose flour
2 teaspoons baking powder
1¼ cups dried fruit (e.g. cherries, apricots, figs), chopped

Put the golden raisins in a bowl to soak with the rum.
Preheat the oven to 425° F.
Thoroughly grease the loaf pan with the butter.
Cream the butter and sugar together in a large bowl. When the mixture turns pale, add the eggs one at a time, stirring constantly.
In another bowl, mix the flour and baking powder, then pour them into the butter mixture in a stream, stirring vigorously with a spatula.
Then stir in the golden raisins and chopped, dried fruit.
Spread the mixture in the pan; put the pan on a baking sheet in the oven, and cook for about 10 minutes. Then lower the temperature to 325° F and cook for another 35 minutes.
Serve warm or cold at teatime.

Coconut and chocolate cake

Serves 4–6
Preparation time: 15 minutes
Cooking time: 45 minutes

1 loaf pan
1 cake rack

1½ tablespoons butter for greasing the pan
4 oz best-quality dark chocolate
2 cups all-purpose flour
1 teaspoon baking powder
2 pinches of salt
3 eggs
½ cup golden superfine sugar
10 tablespoons cooking oil (e.g. sunflower oil)
½ teaspoon vanilla extract
4 tablespoons milk
6 + 2 tablespoons desiccated coconut
4 tablespoons cocoa powder

Preheat the oven to 350° F.
Grease the pan with the butter. Grate the dark chocolate.
Sift the flour and baking powder together into a large bowl. Add a pinch of salt.
Break the eggs, separating the whites from the yolks, and keep them in separate bowls.
Blend the sugar and egg yolks with a whisk.
Pour in the cooking oil, then the flour, stirring all the time, and then the vanilla extract, the milk, the 6 tablespoons desiccated coconut, the cocoa powder, and the grated chocolate.
Add the other pinch of salt to the egg whites and beat them to form peaks, using a whisk. Gently fold them into the mixture using a spatula, making sure they do not break down.
Spread the mixture in the loaf pan. Sprinkle 2 tablespoons desiccated coconut over the top.
Put in the oven. After 10 minutes, lower the oven temperature to 300° F and cook for another 35 minutes or so.
You can tell if it is done by piercing the center with a knife. The blade should come out clean.
Remove the cake from the pan and allow to cool on a cake rack.

Green tea cake

Serves 4–6
Preparation time: 15 minutes
Cooking time: 40 minutes

1 loaf pan
1 cake rack

1 cup all-purpose flour
1 teaspoon baking powder
2 teaspoons green tea powder (available from shops selling Chinese specialties)
2 eggs
1 scant cup confectioners' sugar
½ cup ground almonds
1 stick salted butter (at room temperature), cubed + 1½ tablespoons for greasing the pan
1 pinch of salt

Preheat the oven to 410° F).
Grease the pan with the butter.
Mix the flour, baking powder, and green tea powder in a bowl.
Break the eggs, separating the yolks from the whites. Blend the yolks and confectioners' sugar together in a large bowl, then add the ground almonds.
Then add the cubed butter, blending until the mixture turns smooth.
Put the pinch of salt in with the egg whites, then beat them using the whisk part of your electric mixer, until they form white peaks.
Add the flour, then fold in the egg whites, a little at a time.
Spread the mixture in the pan, put the pan in the oven, and lower the temperature to 325° F. Cook for about 40 minutes
When you take it out of the oven, wait about 10 minutes before removing the cake from the pan, and then leave to cool on a cake rack.

Cherry clafouti

For me, clafouti is no ordinary dish—it takes me back to my childhood!

Serves 4–6
Preparation time: 10 minutes
Cooking time: 30 minutes

1 baking pan

1 lb 5 oz cherries
3 tablespoons salted butter + 1½ tablespoons for greasing the pan
1 cup all-purpose flour
4 tablespoons superfine sugar
1 pinch of salt
1 teaspoon vanilla sugar (see page 12)
4 eggs
1 scant cup milk
confectioners' sugar for decoration

Preheat the oven to 410° F.
Grease the pan generously with the butter.
Quickly wash the cherries under cold running water, remove the stalks, and drain.
Melt the butter in a small, heavy-based saucepan. Combine the flour, sugar, salt, and vanilla sugar in a large bowl.
Break the eggs and blend them with the dry ingredients, a little at a time. Then gradually pour in the milk, still stirring. Add the melted butter. Arrange the cherries in the baking pan and pour the mixture over them.
Bake for 10 minutes in the oven, then lower the temperature to 350° F and cook for another 20 minutes.
Serve the cherry clafouti warm or cold, with a dusting of confectioners' sugar.

Pear clafouti

Serves 4–6
Preparation time: 10 minutes
Cooking time: 30 minutes

1 baking pan

4 ripe pears
3 tablespoons salted butter + 1½ tablespoons for greasing the pan
1 cup all-purpose flour
4 tablespoons superfine sugar
1 pinch of salt
1 pinch of ground cinnamon
1 heaped teaspoon vanilla sugar
4 eggs
1 scant cup milk
4 tablespoons rum
confectioners' sugar for decoration

Preheat the oven to 410° F.
Wash the pears, peel and quarter them; remove the cores and seeds, then slice thinly.
Grease the dish with the butter and arrange the pear slices in the bottom.

Gently melt the butter in a small, heavy-based saucepan.
Mix the flour, sugar, salt, ground cinnamon, and vanilla sugar in a large bowl. Gradually add the whole eggs, then the milk, stirring continuously. Add the melted butter and the rum. The mixture should be quite smooth. Pour it over the pears.
Cook the clafouti in the oven for 10 minutes, then lower the temperature to 350° F and cook for another 20 minutes.
Serve warm or cold, with a dusting of confectioners' sugar.

Apricot clafouti

Serves 4–6
Preparation time: 10 minutes
Cooking time: 30 minutes

1 baking pan

1 lb 5 oz apricots
3 tablespoons salted butter + 1½ tablespoons for greasing the pan
1 cup all-purpose flour
4 tablespoons superfine sugar
1 pinch of salt
1 pinch of ground ginger
1 heaped teaspoon vanilla sugar
4 eggs
1 scant cup milk
confectioners' sugar for decoration

Preheat the oven to 410° F.
Quickly wash the apricots, dry them with a dish towel, then cut them in half. Remove the pits.
Grease the pan with butter and arrange the apricot halves in it, with the flat side facing down.
Gently melt the butter in a small, heavy-based saucepan.
Mix the flour, sugar, salt, ginger, and vanilla sugar in a large bowl. Gradually add the whole eggs and then the milk, stirring all the time. Finally, add the melted butter. The mixture should be quite smooth. Pour it over the apricots.
Put the pan in the oven for 10 minutes, then lower the temperature to 350° F and cook for another 20 minutes.
Serve the apricot clafouti warm or cold, with a dusting of confectioners' sugar.

Cherry clafouti

Breton buttercake (Kouign amann)

Literally 'bread and butter' cake—from Brittany. The secret of a good kouign amann is butter, butter, and yet more butter—and pastry made with bread dough!

Serves 4–6
Preparation time: 10 minutes + 1 hour (for the dough) and 3 x 30 minutes
Cooking time: 30 minutes

1 deep cake pan, about 11 inches in diameter

For the dough:
½ sachet dried yeast
2 tablespoons warm water
a pinch of sugar
2 cups all-purpose flour
For the buttercake:
1 stick salted butter (at room temperature)
½ cup superfine caster sugar + 1½ tablespoons for decoration

In a large bowl , dissolve the yeast in the warm water with a pinch of sugar (or follow the manufacturer's directions on the packet). Sprinkle the flour onto the dissolved yeast and mix to a smooth dough. Cover with a dish towel and leave in a warmish place until it doubles in volume (about 1 hour).
Flatten the dough on your work surface to form a large square. Spread the butter on the dough and dust with sugar. Bring the edges of the dough in towards the center, over the butter and sugar. Roll out the dough again with a rolling pin to make a rectangular shape this time. Fold the bottom third into the centre and the top third over the bottom third. Leave for 30 minutes. Turn the dough through 90° and flatten with the rolling pin. Fold in three again and leave for another 30 minutes.
Turn the pastry through 90° again, fold it, and flatten it with the rolling pin and leave for a further 30 minutes.
Preheat the oven to 410° F. Grease the pan. Using your rolling pin, form the dough into a circle to fit the pan. Put it into the pan, sprinkle it with a little water, and dust with superfine sugar. Cook in the oven for 30 minutes.
Serve warm.

Breton egg plumcake (Far breton)

Serves 4–6
Preparation time: 15 minutes
Cooking time: 30 minutes

1 baking pan

3 cups milk
1 vanilla bean
6 oz prunes, pitted
4 tablespoons all-purpose flour
½ cup superfine sugar
4 eggs
½ stick salted butter + 1½ tablespoons for greasing the pan
1 tablespoon rum

Preheat the oven to 410° F.
Grease an ovenproof pan.
Pour the milk into a heavy-based saucepan. Split the vanilla bean lengthways and put it in the milk. Bring the milk to the boil and immediately take the pan off the heat. Using the point of a knife, scrape the vanilla seeds from inside the bean and put them in the pan along with the empty bean. Leave to infuse as the liquid cools at room temperature.
Arrange the pitted prunes in the pan.
Mix the flour and sugar in a large bowl.
Remove the vanilla bean from the milk, break the eggs, and add them to the milk. Whisk and then add this mixture to the bowl containing the flour and sugar. Melt the butter in a small saucepan and add it to the mixture, with the rum.
Pour the mixture into the dish and cook for about 30 minutes. The cake should turn a nice golden color.
Serve warm or chilled.

TIP • If you would like to soften your prunes and enhance their flavor, soak them for 20 minutes beforehand in a little warm water mixed with rum.

Austrian yeast cake (Kugelhopf)

The secret of a good Kugelhopf lies in the temperature of the ingredients—they must all be at room temperature when you use them. Ideally, you should use a proper Kugelhopf mold, but do not worry if you do not have one—you can get excellent results with an ordinary ring mold.

Serves 4–6
Preparation time: 15 minutes
Cooking time: 50 minutes

1 ring mold

½ cup golden raisins
1 tablespoon water + 2 tablespoons warm water
1 tablespoon kirsch liqueur
1 sachet dried yeast
2½ cups all-purpose flour
4 tablespoons superfine sugar
½ teaspoon salt
10 tablespoons milk
1 egg
1 stick salted butter, cubed, at room temperature + 1½ tablespoons for greasing the mold

Thoroughly grease the mold with the butter.
Soak the golden raisins in the kirsch and 1 tablespoon water in a bowl.
Mix the yeast in 2 tablespoons warm water and leave to swell for about 10 minutes (or follow the directions on the packet).
Put the flour, sugar, salt, milk, yeast, and the egg in the bowl of your food processor and blend vigorously (or use a hand whisk). Add the cubed butter and continue blending until the mixture forms a smooth, pliable dough. Add the golden raisins and mix well.
Spread the dough in the mold, cover with a dish towel, and leave to rise for about 3 hours at room temperature.
Preheat the oven to 410° F. Put the mold in the oven, lower the temperature to 350° F, and leave to cook for about 50 minutes. Remove the Kugelhopf from the mold, and serve cold with coffee or hot chocolate.

TIP • For decoration, you can sprinkle ½ cup whole almonds inside the buttered mold before you put in the dough.

Brioche with pink pralines

Serves 4–6
Preparation time: 25 minutes
Cooking time: 40 minutes

1 loaf pan or brioche mold

1 sachet dried yeast
4 tablespoons warm milk
2 cups all-purpose flour
2 medium eggs + 1 yolk
2 tablespoons superfine sugar
1 stick salted butter (at room temperature),
cubed + 1½ tablespoons for greasing the pan
4 oz pink pralines (candied rose petals)

Dissolve the yeast in the warm milk (or follow the directions on the packet). Pour the flour, eggs, sugar, and yeast mixed with milk into your food processor. Blend on medium speed (or use a hand whisk) then add the cubed butter. Blend again until the mixture is completely smooth.
Form the dough into a ball and put it in a warm place (next to a radiator for instance) covered with a dish towel. Leave it until it doubles in volume (at least 1 hour) then add the pink pralines and knead by hand for a few minutes.
Grease the pan with the butter and put the dough into the pan. Cover once more with the dish towel and leave to rise for 1 hour in a warm place.
Preheat the oven to 350°–375° F
Put the brioche in the oven and cook for about 40 minutes. Ten minutes before the end of the cooking time, lower the oven temperature slightly to prevent the brioche burning on the bottom. Allow to cool slightly before taking the brioche out of the pan.

Butter brioche

Serves 4–6
Preparation time: 20 minutes
Cooking time: 40 minutes

1 loaf pan or brioche mold

1 sachet dried yeast
4 tablespoons warm milk
2 cups all-purpose flour
2 medium eggs + 1 yolk
2 tablespoons superfine sugar
1 stick salted butter (at room temperature),
cubed + 1½ tablespoons for greasing the pan

Dissolve the yeast in the warm milk (or follow the directions on the packet). Pour the flour, eggs, sugar, and yeast in milk into your food processor. Blend on medium speed (or use a hand whisk) then add the cubed butter. Blend again until the mixture is completely smooth.
Form the dough into a ball and put it in a warm place (next to a radiator for instance) covered with a dish towel. Leave until it doubles in volume (at least 1 hour) then knead by hand for a few minutes.
Grease the pan with the butter and put the dough into the pan. Cover once more with the dish towel and leave to rise for 1 hour in a warm place.
Preheat the oven to 350°–375°F.
Put the brioche in the oven and cook for about 40 minutes. Ten minutes before the end of the cooking time, lower the oven temperature slightly to prevent the brioche burning on the bottom. Allow to cool slightly before taking the brioche out of the pan.

Butter brioche

Apple pie

Serves 4–6
Preparation time: 15 minutes
Cooking time: 35 minutes

1 deep cake pan about 9 inches in diameter

1½ tablespoons butter for greasing the pan
1 lb 2 oz shortcrust pastry
2 lb 8 oz good quality eating apples
3 tablespoons golden superfine sugar
1 teaspoon ground cinnamon
1 teaspoon ground ginger
½ teaspoon grated nutmeg
juice of 1 lemon

Preheat the oven to 410° F.
Grease the pan with butter.
Peel and quarter the apples, remove the cores and
seeds, then slice thickly into a large bowl.
Mix the sugar, cinnamon, ginger, and nutmeg
together in a small bowl, then sprinkle over the
apples. Make sure that each piece is dusted with
spiced sugar. Moisten with lemon juice.
Roll out two-thirds of the pastry on a floured
work surface, using a rolling pin. Lift the pastry
into the pan, allowing it to hang over the sides.
Lightly prick the pastry base with a fork. Arrange
the slices of spiced apple on top. Roll out the rest
of the dough into a circle and place over the
apples. Gently press the two thicknesses of pastry
together with the fingers. Make a small hole in
the center of the pastry (to permit steam to
escape during cooking) and put it in the oven for
35 minutes.

TIPS • Serve warm or cold, with vanilla ice cream
or a little cream.
The quantity of sugar used in this recipe
depends on the acidity of your apples. Taste one
raw before you add the sugar!
You can also make delicious pear or rhubarb pies
following the same recipe—substituting pears or
rhubarb for the apples.

Cream cheese cake

Serves 4–6
Preparation time: 15 minutes
Cooking time: 15 minutes + 35 minutes

1 deep cake pan 9 inches in diameter
baking beans

1½ tablespoons butter for greasing the pan
shortcrust pastry (for the base of the pan) (see
page 14)
6 eggs
10 tablespoons superfine sugar
14 oz cream cheese
½ teaspoon vanilla extract
1 pinch of salt
confectioners' sugar

Preheat the oven to 350° F.
Grease the pan and line with shortcrust pastry,
pressing the edges down firmly with the fingertips
and forming a little lip of pastry. Prick the pastry
lightly with a fork. Cover with a layer of baking
beans and cook for 15 minutes in the oven.
Meanwhile, break the eggs and separate the
whites from the yolks. Then mix the sugar and
egg yolks in a large bowl. Add the cream cheese
and vanilla extract.
Add the salt to the egg whites in another bowl
and beat them with your electric whisk until they
form stiff peaks.
Gently fold the egg whites into the cream cheese
mixture with a spatula.
Pour the mixture into the precooked pastry shell
and put in the oven for about 35 minutes.
Remove from the pan and leave to cool on a rack.
Dust the cream cheese cake with a little
confectioners' sugar before serving.

Cheesecake

Serves 6
Preparation time: 10 minutes
Cooking time: 35 minutes

1 deep cake pan 9 inches in diameter

7 oz ginger cookies
½ stick butter (at room temperature), cubed
1 lb 5 oz fresh cream cheese
1 scant cup heavy cream
1 pinch of salt
¾ cup superfine sugar
3 eggs
1 tablespoon maple syrup
1 teaspoon vanilla extract
1 teaspoon ground cinnamon

Preheat the oven to 300° F.
Crush the biscuits and mix them with the butter.
Press the mixture well into the base of the pan.
Beat the cream cheese and cream and add the
salt, sugar, eggs one at a time, maple syrup,
vanilla extract, and cinnamon.
Pour the mixture into the pan and cook in the
oven for about 35 minutes.
Loosen the sides by running a knife blade
between the pan and the cheesecake; leave to
cool, then chill for at least 2 hours.
This cheesecake can be made the day before.

Tarts, charlottes, etc.

Lemon tart

Serves 4–6
Preparation time: 25 minutes
Cooking time: 20 minutes

1 tart pan 10 inches in diameter
baking beans

10½ oz sweet flan pastry (see page 14)
4 sheets of gelatin
juice and rind of 4 unwaxed lemons
1¾ cups superfine sugar
8 fresh eggs
2¼ sticks salted butter (at room temperature),
cubed + 1½ tablespoons for greasing the pan

Preheat the oven to 350° F.
Put the sheets of gelatin to soak in a bowl of cold water.
Grease the pan with the butter. Roll out the pastry and line the pan with it.
Prick the pastry base lightly with a fork and cover with a sheet of waxed paper. Sprinkle some baking beans on top and cook for 10 to 12 minutes.
Beat the eggs.
Remove the beans and the waxed paper, glaze the pastry with a little of the beaten egg, and put back in the oven for another 5 minutes or so. This will keep the pastry crisp when filled with the lemon cream. Take the tart shell out of the pan and leave to cool on a rack.
Pour the juice and rind of the lemons, superfine sugar, eggs, and cubed butter into a heavy-based saucepan. Mix well and boil for 1 minute. Add the gelatin leaves, whisk, and pour the mixture into the tart shell.
Leave to cool before serving.

Tropical fruit tart

Serves 4–6
Preparation time: 20 minutes
Cooking time: 15 minutes

1 tart pan about 10 inches in diameter
baking beans
1 cake rack

1½ tablespoons butter for greasing the pan
10½ oz shortcrust pastry (see page 14)
2 bananas
3 kiwi fruit
1 fresh pineapple
1¼ cups light cream
9 oz crème pâtissière (see page 18)

Preheat the oven to 350° F.
Thoroughly grease the pan.
Roll the pastry and cut out a circle to line the pan.
Prick the base lightly with a fork and cover with a sheet of waxed paper. Sprinkle some baking beans on top and cook for about 15 minutes.
Meanwhile, prepare the fruit. Peel them; slice the bananas and kiwi fruit, and cut the pineapple into cubes.
Take the cream out of the refrigerator and whisk lightly. Fold it into the crème pâtissière.
Remove the tart shell from the oven when done, take it out of the pan, and leave to cool on a rack.
Spread a layer of crème pâtissière over the pastry and arrange the fruit on top.

TIP • To make this tart even more delicious, you could heat 2 tablespoons apple jello with a tablespoon of water and use it to glaze the fruit with a brush.

Lemon tart

Apricot and almond tart

Serves 4–6
Preparation time: 35 minutes
Cooking time: 30 minutes

1 tart pan approximately 10 inches in diameter
baking beans

1 pinch of salt
4 tablespoons cold water + 4 tablespoons for
cooking the apricots
2 cups all-purpose flour
1 tablespoon sugar
½ cup cooking oil
1 tablespoon orange flower water
1½ tablespoons butter for greasing the pan
10 apricots
1 tablespoon honey
1 cup ground almonds
½ cup flaked almonds

First make the pastry: dissolve the salt in 4
tablespoons cold water. Mix the flour with the
sugar and oil. Add the salted water and the
orange flower water and knead the pastry with
the fingertips. Cover with plastic wrap and leave
in the refrigerator for at least 1 hour.
Preheat the oven to 350° F.
Lightly grease the pan with the butter. Line it with
the pastry and prick lightly with a fork. Cover
with a circle of waxed paper and a layer of dried
beans. Put the tart shell in the oven for about 15
minutes.
Meanwhile, wash the apricots, dry them, cut
them in half, and remove the pits.
Pour the water and honey into a skillet. Carefully
place the apricot halves in the water and cook
them for about 15 minutes, turning them over
half way through.
Take the tart shell out of the pan and leave to
cool, then cover with a layer of ground almonds.
Place the halved, cooked apricots face down in
the shell. Sprinkle with flaked almonds and serve
immediately.

TIP • You do not need to wait for the summer to
make this tart. You can always use frozen
apricots.

Plum tart with cinnamon

If you can get it, the Alsatian quetsch is a wonder-
ful plum for cooking. It gives off a subtle aroma of
caramel when ripe. You could also use the Czar or
Kirke's Blue varieties.

Serves 4–6
Preparation time: 20 minutes
Cooking time: 35 minutes

1 tart pan about 10 inches in diameter

9 oz shortcrust pastry (see page 14)
1½ tablespoons butter for greasing the pan
2 lb 12 oz plums
1 cup ground almonds
6 tablespoons golden superfine sugar
½ teaspoon ground cinnamon

Preheat the oven to 350° F.
Grease the pan and line it with the pastry. Pinch
the edges with your fingers. Lightly prick the tart
base with a fork. Cover with a layer of plastic
wrap and put in the refrigerator for about 15
minutes.
Wash the plums, dry them thoroughly, then cut
them in half and remove the pits.
Sprinkle a layer of ground almonds in the tart
shell and arrange the plums on top, cut face up.
Mix the sugar and cinnamon in a bowl, then
sprinkle this spicy mixture over the plums.
Cook for about 35 minutes. Remove from the pan
and allow the tart to cool a little.
Serve with vanilla ice cream.

Upside-down cake (Tarte Tatin)

This upside-down cake has many different versions. Here are three to choose from. You can also make up your own but apple tarte Tatin made with cooking apples will always be the best.

Upside-down cake (Tarte Tatin)—with apples

Serves 4–6
Preparation time: 10 minutes
Cooking time: 30 minutes

1 deep baking pan about 9 inches in diameter

10½ oz shortcrust pastry (see page 14)
2 lb 4 oz cooking apples
½ cup superfine sugar
3 tablespoons water
vinegar
3 tablespoons salted butter (at room temperature), cubed (for the caramel) + 1½ tablespoons for greasing the pan + 1½ tablespoons for the apples

Preheat the oven to 475° F. Grease the pan with butter.
Peel and quarter the apples, and remove the cores and seeds. Cut them into chunks.

Make the caramel: slowly dissolve 4 tablespoons sugar with 3 tablespoons water in a small, heavy-based saucepan. Then turn up the heat and boil until the mixture turns golden; add 2 or 3 drops of white or malt vinegar and 3 tablespoons butter. Remove from the heat, stir, and pour into the buttered pan.
Arrange the apple chunks in the pan, rounded side down, and dot with butter. Dust with the remaining sugar.
Roll the pastry out to form a large circle, place it on top of the apples, and tuck in the edges. Cook for about 25 minutes.

TIP • Serve the tart warm, or reheat it slightly. If you reheat it in a microwave, do not leave it in too long as the pastry may lose its crispness. Always serve with a small jug of cream for each guest.

Upside-down cake (Tarte Tatin)–with mangoes

Serves 4–6
Preparation time: 10 minutes
Cooking time: 30 minutes

1 deep baking pan about 9 inches in diameter

10½ oz shortcrust pastry (see page 14)
2 lb 4 oz mangoes
½ cup superfine sugar
3 tablespoons water
vinegar
3 tablespoons salted butter (at room temperature), cubed (for the caramel) + 1½ tablespoons for the mangoes

Preheat the oven to 475° F.
Grease the pan with butter.
Peel the mangoes, remove the pits, and cut into slices.
Make the caramel: slowly dissolve 4 tablespoons sugar with 3 tablespoons water in a small, heavy-based saucepan. Then turn up the heat and boil until the mixture turns golden; add 2 or 3 drops of white or malt vinegar and 3 tablespoons butter. Remove from the heat, stir, and pour into the buttered pan.
Arrange the mangoes in the pan on top of the caramel. Dust with the remaining sugar and dot with the cubed butter.
Roll the pastry to form a large circle; place it on top of the mangoes and tuck in the edges. Cook for about 25 minutes.
Serve warm.

Upside-down cake (Tarte Tatin)–with pears

Serves 4–6
Preparation time: 10 minutes
Cooking time: 30 minutes

1 deep baking pan about 9 inches in diameter

10½ oz shortcrust pastry (see page 14)
2 lb 4 oz firm pears
½ cup superfine sugar
3 tablespoons water
vinegar
3 tablespoons salted butter (at room temperature), cubed (for the caramel) + 1½ tablespoons for the pears

Preheat the oven to 475° F.
Grease the pan with the butter.
Peel and quarter the pears, and remove the cores and seeds. Cut them into chunks.
Make the caramel: slowly dissolve 4 tablespoons sugar with 3 tablespoons water in a small, heavy-based saucepan. Then turn up the heat and boil until the mixture turns golden; add 2 or 3 drops of white or malt vinegar and 3 tablespoons butter. Remove from the heat, stir, and pour into the buttered pan.
Arrange the pear chunks in the dish, rounded side down, and dot with butter. Dust with the remaining sugar.
Roll the pastry out to form a large circle, place it on top of the pears, and tuck in the edges. Cook for about 25 minutes.
Serve warm.

Upside-down cake with pears

Strawberry tart

Some good quality shortcrust pastry, some tasty strawberries, and some homemade crème Chantilly! It is as easy as that. Sheer bliss!

Serves 4–6
Preparation time: 15 minutes
Cooking time: 15 minutes

1 tart pan about 10 inches in diameter
baking beans
1 cake rack

10½ oz shortcrust pastry (see page 14)
1½ tablespoons butter for greasing the pan
1 lb strawberries
1 scant cup heavy cream
½ teaspoon vanilla sugar

Preheat the oven to 350° F.
Thoroughly grease the pan.
Roll out the pastry to form a large circle and line the pan with it. Make a little rim all around. Lightly prick the base with a fork, cover it with a sheet of waxed paper, and place some baking beans on top. Cook for about 15 minutes.
When cooked but not colored, take the tart shell out of the oven; remove the waxed paper and the baking beans. Take the tart shell out of the pan and leave to cool on a rack.
Prepare the strawberries: wash them quickly under cold running water, drain, and hull them. Cut them in half. Arrange the strawberries on the tart shell, cut side up.

Crème Chantilly

See recipe page 22.

Decorate the tart with blobs of cream. You can use a frosting bag if you like. Serve immediately.

Raspberry tart

Make your tart shell exactly as for the strawberry tart. Make the crème Chantilly in advance and keep it in the refrigerator.
Just before serving, spread a layer of crème Chantilly in the tart shell and arrange the fresh raspberries on top.

VARIATIONS • According to the season, you can replace the raspberries with blackberries or blackcurrants. Not only are these tarts good to eat—they look pretty too.
You can often find good quality frozen fruit in specialist shops. Remember to thaw it well in advance.

Austrian shortbread (Linzertorte)

Serves 4–6
Preparation time: 20 minutes
Cooking time: 30 minutes

1 tart pan about 10 inches in diameter

1 cup all-purpose flour
1 pinch of salt
1 egg
1 stick salted butter (at room temperature),
cubed + 1½ tablespoons for greasing the pan
½ cup superfine sugar
1 cup ground almonds
grated rind of ¼ unwaxed lemon
1 teaspoon ground cinnamon
1 teaspoon cocoa powder
10 tablespoons raspberry jelly
milk to glaze

Sift the flour onto the work surface and make a well in the middle. Put the salt, egg, butter, and sugar in the well. Mix using your fingertips then add the ground almonds, lemon rind, cinnamon, and cocoa powder. Gradually blend in the flour, then quickly work the pastry between the thumbs and fingertips until it takes on a sandy texture.
Roll it into a ball, wrap in plastic wrap, and put in the refrigerator for at least 1 hour.
Preheat the oven to 350° F.
Grease the pan.
Roll two-thirds of the pastry out into a circle, roll it round the rolling pin, and press it gently into the pan.
Spread the jelly over the pastry base, then roll out the rest of the pastry and cut it into strips ½ inch wide (as illustrated above left). Arrange the strips in a lattice over the jelly. Glaze with a little milk and cook for 30 minutes.
Serve cold with whipped cream. The pastry is best if made the day before.

Almond tartlets

Makes 8 tartlets
Preparation time: 15 minutes
Cooking time: 20 minutes

Tartlet pans 4 inches in diameter

10½ oz shortcrust pastry (see page 14)
1 cup ground almonds
3 eggs
3 tablespoons salted butter (at room
temperature), cubed + 1½ tablespoons for
greasing the pans
2 tablespoons superfine sugar
1 tablespoon rum

Preheat the oven to 350° F.
Thoroughly grease the pans with the butter.
Mix the ground almonds with the eggs, butter,
sugar, and rum.
Roll out the shortcrust pastry and cut into circles
about 6 inches in diameter.
Put a circle of pastry into each pan, gently
pressing it in with the fingers. Then prick the base
of each tartlet with a fork.
Spread the almond mixture over the pastry and
cook for about 20 minutes.
If you like, you can decorate the tartlets with
flaked, roasted almonds.

Apple cobbler

Serves 4–6
Preparation time: 15 minutes
Cooking time: 35 minutes

1 baking pan

2 lb 12 oz apples
4 tablespoons calvados
1 cup whole-wheat flour (or half whole-wheat,
half all-purpose flour)
½ cup ground almonds
1 teaspoon ground cinnamon
½ cup golden superfine sugar
1 stick salted butter (at room temperature),
cubed + 1½ tablespoons for greasing the pan
1 pinch of salt

Preheat the oven to 350° F.
Grease the pan with butter.
Peel and quarter the apples, remove the cores and
seeds, and slice coarsely.
Put the apples on a deep plate and drizzle with
calvados.
Mix the flour, ground almonds, cinnamon, sugar,
and butter in a large bowl. Add the pinch of salt.
Stir gently.
Arrange the apple slices soaked in calvados in the
dish. Cover with the flour-ground-almond-butter-
sugar mixture and cook for about 35 minutes
Serve warm or cold.

Red fruit cobbler

Serves 4–6
Preparation time: 15 minutes
Cooking time: 25 minutes

1 baking pan

1 lb 12 oz red fruit (raspberries, redcurrants,
blackcurrants, blackberries, etc.)
1 cup all-purpose flour
½ cup golden superfine sugar
½ cup ground almonds
½ teaspoon ground cinnamon
1 stick salted butter (at room temperature),
cubed + 1½ tablespoons for greasing the pan
1 pinch of salt
grated rind of ½ an unwaxed lemon

Preheat the oven to 350° F.
Grease the pan with butter.
Pick over the fruit, then wash it quickly under cold
running water and drain.
Combine the flour, sugar, ground almonds,
cinnamon, and butter in a large bowl.
Add the pinch of salt. Rub together with the
fingertips until the mixture resembles
breadcrumbs.
Sprinkle the lemon rind over the base of the pan
and arrange the red fruits on top. Cover with the
flour-sugar-ground-almond-cinnamon-butter
mixture and cook for about 25 minutes.
Serve warm or cold.

Rhubarb and apple cobbler

Serves 4–6
Preparation time: 15 minutes
Cooking time: 25 minutes

1 baking pan

3 apples
2 lb 4 oz rhubarb, cut into chunks
½ cup golden superfine sugar for the fruit + 6
tablespoons for the cobbler
½ teaspoon ground ginger
1 cup all-purpose flour
1 stick salted butter (at room temperature),
cubed + 1½ tablespoons for greasing the pan
1 pinch of salt

Preheat the oven to 350° F.
Grease the pan with butter.
Peel and quarter the apples, remove the cores and
seeds, and slice coarsely. Put the slices in a large
bowl with the prepared rhubarb, sugar, and
ginger. Mix well.
Combine the flour, the remaining 6 tablespoons
sugar and butter in a large bowl. Add the pinch
of salt. Rub together with the fingertips until the
mixture resembles breadcrumbs.
Arrange the apples and rhubarb in the dish. Cover
with the flour-butter-sugar mixture and cook for
about 25 minutes.
Serve warm or cold.
For a pleasant, nutty flavor, try using whole-wheat
flour.

Rhubarb and apple cobbler

Red fruit cobbler

Mango and cinnamon charlotte

Make the day before
Serves 4–6
Preparation time: 15 minutes
Cooking time: 20 minutes

1 charlotte mold with removable lid or a straight-sided, glass dish

1 lb 12 oz mangoes (fresh or tinned)
2 tablespoons salted butter
6 tablespoons superfine sugar + 4 tablespoons for the caramel
½ teaspoon ground cinnamon
4 tablespoons water
1 cup milk
30 sponge fingers

The day before, peel the mangoes, remove the pits, and chop the flesh.
Melt the butter in a nonstick skillet and use it to cook the chopped mangoes on a medium heat for a few minutes. Pour in 6 tablespoons sugar and cook on a low heat for about 12 minutes. Then add the ground cinnamon and mix well.
Make the caramel: melt 4 tablespoons sugar with 2 tablespoons water in a small, heavy-based saucepan. Then boil rapidly until the caramel turns a golden color. Remove from the heat and pour in 2 tablespoons of water. Leave to cool, then add the milk.
Quickly dip the sponge fingers in the caramelized milk and use them to line the base and sides of the mold.
Put a layer of mango in the base and cover it with dipped fingers; fill the mold with alternate layers, finishing with a layer of fingers.
Serve with custard, if you like.

Pear charlotte

Make the day before
Serves 4–6
Preparation time: 15 minutes
Cooking time: 20 minutes

1 charlotte mold with removable lid or a straight-sided, glass dish

1 lb 12 oz pears
2 tablespoons salted butter
6 tablespoons superfine sugar + 4 tablespoons for the caramel
2 heaped teaspoons vanilla sugar
2 tablespoons water
1 cup milk
30 sponge fingers

The day before, peel and quarter the pears, remove the cores and seeds, and slice.
Melt the butter in a nonstick skillet and use it to cook the pears on medium heat for a few minutes. Pour in the 6 tablespoons superfine sugar and the vanilla sugar, and cook on a very low heat for about 12 minutes.
Make the caramel: melt 4 tablespoons sugar with 2 tablespoons water in a small, heavy-based saucepan. Then boil rapidly until the caramel turns a golden color. Remove from the heat and pour in 2 tablespoons of water. Leave to cool, then add the milk.
Quickly dip the sponge fingers in the caramelized milk and use them to line the base and sides of the mold. Put a layer of pears in the bottom and cover them with dipped fingers. Continue with alternate layers until the mold is full, finishing with a layer of fingers.
Cover the mold and put it in the refrigerator overnight. Take the charlotte out of the mold and serve very cold.
If you like, you can pour on some hot caramel, just before serving.

Pear charlotte

Red fruit charlotte

Make the day before
Serves 4–6
Preparation time: 15 minutes
No cooking required

1 charlotte mold with removable lid or a straight-sided, glass dish

30 sponge fingers
10 tablespoons orange juice
14 oz fromage frais
6 tablespoons superfine sugar
2 heaped teaspoons vanilla sugar (see page 12)
10½ oz raspberries and strawberries
a few blackcurrants for decoration

Quickly dip the sponge fingers in the orange juice. Use them to line the base and sides of the mold. Whisk the fromage frais, sugar, and vanilla sugar in a bowl.
Quickly wash the raspberries and strawberries under cold running water and drain them. Put half the red fruit in the mold and cover with half the sweetened fromage frais. Add a layer of sponge fingers followed by the remaining red fruit and fromage frais. Finish with a layer of sponge fingers.
Cover and chill in the refrigerator overnight. Remove from the mold and serve very cold.

Chocolate charlotte

Make the day before
Serves 4–6
Preparation time: 15 minutes
No cooking required

1 charlotte mold with removable lid or a straight-sided, glass dish

1 lb 5 oz dark chocolate mousse (see page 150)
1 cup black coffee
3 tablespoons brandy
30 sponge fingers

The day before, pour the coffee and brandy into a shallow dish. Quickly dip the fingers into the liquid and use them to line the base and sides of the mold.
Fill with chocolate mousse and top with a layer of fingers.
Cover and chill in the refrigerator overnight. Remove the charlotte from the mold and serve very cold.
If you like you can decorate the charlotte with sifted cocoa powder just before serving and serve with custard.
You could also flavor the chocolate mousse with the grated rind of an unwaxed orange.

Chocolate charlotte

Raspberry Swiss roll

THIS CAKE NEVER FAILS TO IMPRESS. If you follow the recipe in stages, you will find it easy to make. You can of course use different jellies for the filling.

Serves 4
Preparation time: 15 minutes
Cooking time: 15 minutes

1 Swiss roll pan approximately 12 x 9 inches

1½ tablespoons butter for greasing the pan
3 eggs
½ cup superfine sugar
2 tablespoons all-purpose flour
4 tablespoons cornstarch
1 pinch of salt
12 oz jar raspberry jelly
confectioners' sugar for decoration

Preheat the oven to 300° F.
Grease the pan and line it with waxed paper.
Separate the eggs. Put the whites in a large bowl. Combine the yolks with the sugar in a basin. Beat until the mixture turns pale and frothy. Add the flour and cornstarch and mix well.
Add the pinch of salt to the egg whites and, with a whisk, beat until they form stiff peaks. Gently fold them into the yolk-sugar mixture using a spatula.
Pour the mixture into the pan. If necessary, smooth the top with a spatula to ensure even distribution. Put in the oven to cook for about 15 minutes.
As soon as it comes out of the oven, turn the sponge out onto a damp cloth and roll it up quickly in the cloth. Then unroll it and spread with a layer of raspberry jelly. Roll up again in the cloth as tightly as possible. Leave to cool.
Remove the cloth, dust the cake with a little confectioners' sugar and serve.

Yuletide chocolate log

NOWADAYS, YOU CAN BUY THESE IN CAKE SHOPS. There is just one problem: you miss out on the pleasure—and the satisfaction—of making your own Christmas cake.

Serves 6–8
Preparation time: 45 minutes
Cooking time: 20 minutes

1 baking sheet lined with waxed paper

For the sponge

½ cup superfine sugar
1½ cups ground almonds
4 tablespoons all-purpose flour
4 whole eggs + 5 whites
2 tablespoons salted butter (at room temperature), cubed
1 pinch of salt
½ cup chopped hazelnuts
confectioners' sugar

For the syrup

6 tablespoons superfine sugar
6 tablespoons water
4 tablespoons rum

For the chocolate ganache

1¼ cups light cream
14 oz best-quality dark chocolate, grated
6 tablespoons butter (at room temperature), cubed

Preheat the oven to 410° F.

Using your electric mixer (or a hand whisk), combine the sugar, ground almonds, flour, whole eggs, and cubed butter.

Add the salt to the egg whites and beat them to form stiff peaks. Fold into the sponge mixture using a spatula.

Spread the mixture on the baking sheet. Sprinkle the chopped hazelnuts on top. Cook for 5–8 minutes.

Meanwhile make the syrup: slowly melt the sugar in the water and rum in a small, heavy-based saucepan. Moisten the sponge with this syrup using a pastry brush.

Next make the ganache: pour the cream into a heavy-based saucepan, bring to the boil, and pour it onto the grated chocolate. Stir with a spoon, then add the cubed butter and mix until completely smooth.

Spread a layer of ganache over the sponge and roll up. Spread ganache on the top. Use a fork to make streaks on the chocolate.

Dust with a little confectioners' sugar.

Twelfth Night cake with frangipane

According to tradition, whoever gets the slice containing the dried bean becomes king and may choose a queen (or vice versa).

Serves 4–6
Preparation time: 15 minutes
Cooking time: 25 minutes

1 baking sheet lined with waxed paper

2 sheets ready-made puff pastry
½ cup superfine sugar
1 stick salted butter (at room temperature), cubed
3 whole eggs + 1 yolk
few drops of vanilla extract
4 tablespoons all-purpose flour
1½ cups ground almonds
1 dried bean

Preheat the oven to 410° F.
First make the frangipane: beat the sugar and cubed butter until the mixture turns pale and slightly frothy. Add the whole eggs one at a time, while continuing to beat. Then add the vanilla extract.
Combine the flour and ground almonds in a bowl and add them to the butter-sugar-egg mixture.
Roll out one sheet of puff pastry. Spread it with the frangipane, leaving a margin of about 1¼ inches.
Put the dried bean in the frangipane.
Moisten the edges of the pastry with a little water then cover with the other sheet of puff pastry, pressing the edges together neatly with your fingers.
Glaze the top of the cake with beaten egg yolk and make a criss-cross pattern with the point of a knife. Take care not to pierce the pastry.
Cook for about 25 minutes.
Now all you have to do is find the king!

Fruit desserts and puddings

Harvest pie

Serves 6
Preparation time: 20 minutes
Cooking time: 40 minutes

1 baking sheet lined with waxed paper

1 lb 2 oz shortcrust pastry (see page 14)
4 lb 8 oz firm pears
juice of 1 lemon
4 tablespoons golden superfine sugar
2 pinches root ginger, freshly grated
1 egg yolk

Peel and halve the pears; remove the cores and
seeds. Cut into thick slices. Sprinkle with lemon
juice.
Mix the sugar and ginger together in a bowl. Pour
this mixture over the pears and mix gently using
your fingers, to give an even distribution.
Roll out the pastry to make a circle about 14
inches in diameter on the baking sheet.
Arrange the slices of pear over half the pastry,
leaving a ¾ inch margin. Fold the other half of the
pastry over the pears and seal the edges, using
your fingers to make a hem.
Whisk the egg yolk in a bowl and use it to glaze
the surface of the pastry.
Cook in the oven for about 40 minutes.

TIP • You can just as easily use apples instead of
pears.

Apples baked with honey and spices

Serves 6
Preparation time: 15 minutes
Cooking time: 35 minutes

1 baking pan

6 apples
6 teaspoons honey
1½ tablespoons butter
1 pinch ground nutmeg
1 pinch ground cinnamon
2 tablespoons water

Preheat the oven to 350° F.
Wash the apples and dry them thoroughly with a
clean towel. Take out the cores and seeds using
an apple corer or a knife. Put the apples in a dish
and pour 1 teaspoon of honey over each. Put a
knob of butter into each cavity and dust with the
nutmeg and cinnamon. Pour 2 tablespoons of
water into the bottom of the dish and cook for
about 35 minutes.
Baste the apples frequently with their cooking
liquid to prevent them drying out.
Serve warm or cold.

You could pour half a glass of white wine into the
pan with the water. In cooking the wine becomes
concentrated and gives the syrup a delicious
flavor.

TIP • Preferably use cooking apples.

Apples baked with honey and spices

Caramelized apples

Serves 4–6
Preparation time: 25 minutes
Cooking time: 35 minutes

1 charlotte mold or glass bowl, or individual molds

1½ tablespoons butter for greasing the mold(s)
½ cup superfine sugar + 4 tablespoons for the caramel
2 tablespoons water + 1 teaspoon boiling water + 1 glass water
2–3 drops vinegar
3 lb 5 oz apples
½ teaspoon ground cinnamon
3 eggs

Preheat the oven to 350° F.
Grease the mold with butter.
Slowly dissolve 4 tablespoons of sugar with 2 tablespoons of water in a heavy-based saucepan. When the mixture turns golden, add 2 or 3 drops of vinegar and take the pan off the heat. Add 1 teaspoon boiling water and stir.
Pour this caramel into the mold, tipping and turning the mold in order to coat the sides and base. Leave to cool, then butter the inside of the mold where not coated with caramel.
Peel and quarter the apples; remove the cores and seeds. Add a glass of water to the pan and cook them in a heavy-based saucepan on a high heat. Stir frequently to reduce the liquid, then take off the heat and add ½ cup sugar and the cinnamon. Stir well. While the apples are still warm, add the eggs one at a time, beating constantly. Pour this mixture into the caramelized mold.
Half fill a baking pan with boiling water, stand the mold in the water, and cook in the oven for about 15–20 minutes.
Leave to cool, and take out of the mold just before serving.

Apple and caramel compote

It cannot be overemphasized: for a good compote you need good quality fruit! No windfalls and no bruised or damaged fruit!

Serves 6
Preparation time: 15 minutes
Cooking time: 50 minutes

2½ cups superfine sugar
1 glass water
4 lb 8 oz cooking apples
2 tablespoons calvados
1 small container heavy cream

Slowly dissolve 1 scant cup of sugar in a glass of water in a heavy-based saucepan, stirring with a spatula until the mixture turns golden brown. Remove the pan from the heat.
Peel and quarter the apples; remove the cores and seeds. Mix them with the remaining sugar then put the quartered apples in the pan and cook very slowly, stirring frequently to prevent burning. You can add a tablespoon of water if they dry out too much.
Blend the cooked compote in your food processor to make it smoother. Pour in the calvados and leave to cool.
Serve the apple and caramel compote very cold with a dollop of cream.

Apple and caramel compote

Summer pudding

Serves 4–6
Preparation time: 20 minutes
Cooking time: 5 minutes
Chill overnight

1 charlotte mold or glass bowl

14 oz raspberries
5 oz redcurrants
5 oz blackberries
10 tablespoons superfine sugar
8–10 slices brioche (or white bread)
1½ tablespoons butter

Grease the mold.
Quickly rinse the fruit under cold running water
and drain.
Put it in a pan with the sugar and bring to the
boil. Leave to simmer for about 5 minutes.
Press the slices of bread against the sides and
base of the mold. Put the red fruit into the mold,
filling it to the top. Keep any leftover fruit for
decoration. Then cover with bread.
Put a small plate on top and place something
heavy on top of the plate to weigh it down.
Leave the pudding in the refrigerator overnight.
To serve, turn it out on to a serving plate and
decorate with the leftover fruit and a little cream.

Bread pudding with red fruit

Serves 4–6
Preparation time: 10 minutes
Cooking time: 8 minutes

2 eggs
½ cup confectioners' sugar
2 cups milk
2 knobs butter
1 tablespoon cooking oil
8 thick slices of stale white bread (or brioche)
10 oz red fruit (strawberries, redcurrants,
blackcurrants etc.)

Break the eggs into a shallow dish, add the sugar,
and beat with a fork.
Pour the milk into a deep-sided dish.
Heat 1 knob of butter and 1 tablespoon of
cooking oil in a skillet.
Quickly dip the slices of bread in the milk and
then in the beaten egg, and put them in the
skillet. Let them brown a little, then turn them
over.
Heat the other knob of butter in another frying
pan, tip in the red fruit, and heat slowly while
stirring.
Serve the bread pudding with the red fruit and a
dusting of confectioners' sugar.

Bread pudding with red fruit

Lemon pudding

Serves 4–6
Preparation time: 10 minutes
Cooking time: 30 minutes

1 deep baking pan about 9 inches in diameter

1½ tablespoons butter for greasing the pan
4 eggs
¾ cup superfine sugar
2 heaped teaspoons vanilla sugar
1 lb 2 oz fromage frais
grated rind of 1 lemon
1 pinch of salt

Preheat the oven to 335° F.
Grease the pan with the butter.
Separate the eggs. Beat the egg yolks with the superfine sugar and the vanilla sugar until the mixture turns creamy. Add the fromage frais and the grated lemon rind.
Add the pinch of salt to the egg whites and beat with a whisk to form stiff peaks. Gently fold them into the egg yolk-sugar mixture.
Spread the mixture in the pan and cook for about 30 minutes. Leave the pudding to cool in the dish and serve cold.

Rice cake

Serves 4
Preparation time: 5 minutes
Cooking time: 1 hour 10 minutes

1 ovenproof pudding basin

1¼ cups round-grain rice
8 cups milk
1 vanilla bean
6 tablespoons superfine sugar + 4 tablespoons for the caramel
4 egg yolks
3 tablespoons water
1 drop of lemon juice

Quickly wash the rice under cold running water.
Pour the milk into a heavy-based saucepan and add the vanilla bean split in two lengthways.
Bring to the boil and pour in the rice.
Cover and leave to simmer for about 35 minutes.
Five minutes before the end of the cooking time, add 6 tablespoons sugar and stir well. When done, remove the vanilla bean, pour the rice into a basin, pour in the egg yolks, and mix well.
Preheat the oven to 350° F.
Dissolve 4 tablespoons sugar in 3 tablespoons of water in a heavy-based saucepan and cook, stirring with a spatula until the mixture turns golden. Remove the saucepan from the heat, add a drop of lemon juice, and stir once.
Pour the caramel into the mold and swirl it round to coat the sides, then add the cooked rice. Bake in the oven for about 35 minutes. The top of the pudding should turn an attractive amber color. Allow to cool before turning it out of the dish.

Prunes in red wine and cinnamon

A quick dessert that can be made in advance. It will take a weight off your mind!

Serves 4–6
Preparation time: 35 minutes
Cooking time 10 minutes

1 lb 12 oz prunes
4 tablespoons brandy
1 vanilla bean
6 cups red wine
½ cup superfine sugar
1 cinnamon stick
1 clove
1 pinch of ground ginger

Put the prunes and brandy in a large bowl to soak for half an hour.
Split the vanilla bean lengthways.
Put the wine, sugar, cinnamon stick, vanilla pod, clove, and ground ginger in a heavy-based saucepan. Bring to the boil and add the prunes together with any liquid from the bottom of the bowl.
Bring to the boil again and leave to simmer for another 5 minutes.
Then take off the heat and leave the prunes to cool in their spicy syrup.
This dish tastes even better if made the day before.

Rice pudding

A very easy recipe that can be enhanced with grated orange or lemon rind.

Serves 4
Preparation time: 5 minutes
Cooking time: 45 minutes

1¼ cups round-grain rice
8 cups milk
1 vanilla bean
6 tablespoons superfine sugar

Quickly wash the rice in cold water. Put the milk into a heavy-based saucepan and add the vanilla bean split lengthways. Bring to the boil and pour in the rice. Cover and simmer for about 45 minutes. Five minutes before the end of cooking, add the sugar and stir well. When cooked, remove the vanilla bean, pour the rice into a basin, and leave to cool at room temperature.

TIP • Do not stir the rice during the cooking process.

Chocolate mousse

The dessert that everyone adores. You can also use this mousse to fill meringues, pancakes, or a charlotte shell.

Serves 4–6
Preparation time: 10 minutes
Cooking time: 8 minutes

Individual ramekin dishes or a large bowl

7 oz best-quality dark chocolate
6 fresh eggs
¾ cup confectioners' sugar
1 pinch of salt

Break the chocolate into pieces.
Heat some water in a saucepan. Put the chocolate in a bowl with a tablespoon of water and stand the bowl in the saucepan. Slowly melt the chocolate. The water should not be allowed to boil, just simmer. Take the bowl of chocolate off the heat and stir with a spoon.
Separate the eggs. Mix the egg yolks and the sugar and pour this mixture into the melted chocolate.
Add the salt to the egg whites and beat to form stiff peaks using an electric mixer (or a hand whisk). Gently fold them into the eggs-sugar-chocolate mixture, using a spatula to ensure that the egg whites are thoroughly blended, taking care not to let them break down.
Divide the mixture between the ramekin dishes. Cover with plastic wrap and put the mousse in the refrigerator for about 2 hours.
Serve cold.

TIP • You can flavor the mousse with 1 tablespoon of brandy or rum and serve with Cats' tongues (Langues de chat) (see page 38).

Chocolate fondant

Serves 4–6
Preparation time: 10 minutes
Cooking time: 8 minutes
Make the day before

1 soufflé dish or charlotte mold, greased with butter

12 oz best-quality dark chocolate
1 tablespoon water
4 eggs
1½ sticks butter (at room temperature), cubed + 1½ tablespoons for greasing the dish
½ cup superfine sugar
1 pinch of salt

Grease the dish with butter.
Break the chocolate into pieces.
Heat some water in a saucepan. Put the chocolate in a bowl with a tablespoon of water and stand the bowl in the saucepan. Slowly melt the chocolate. The water should not be allowed to boil, just simmer.
Separate the eggs.
Mix the butter and sugar in a bowl until the mixture turns creamy. Then pour in the melted chocolate, mix well, and add the egg yolks one at a time, stirring continuously.
Add the salt to the egg whites and beat them to form stiff peaks using an electric mixer (or a hand whisk). Fold them gently into the eggs-sugar-chocolate mixture using a spatula to ensure that the egg whites are thoroughly blended, taking care not to let them break down.
Pour the mixture into the dish.
Cover the top with plastic wrap and refrigerate overnight.
Remove from the dish just before serving.
It should be eaten very cold.
You may wish to dust the fondant with confectioners' sugar.

Chocolate fondant

Orange and almond gratin

A very sophisticated dish but one that is neverthe-less easy to make. You can use the same basic recipe to make strawberry or peach gratins, etc.

Serves 4
Preparation time: 25 minutes
Cooking time: 10 minutes

1 small baking pan

3 oranges
3 tablespoons butter (at room temperature), cubed + 1½ tablespoons for greasing the pan
¾ cup confectioners' sugar
¾ cup ground almonds
1 egg
½ cup whipping cream

Grease the pan with butter.
Wash and dry the oranges. Remove the peel and cut the oranges into thick slices. Carefully remove the white pith.
Preheat the broiler section of your oven to 410° F.
Make the almond cream: put the cubed butter in a large bowl. Pour in the confectioners' sugar and ground almonds; mix well.
Add the egg and mix again.
Pour the cream into another bowl and whip vigorously. Pour the whipped cream into the almond cream mixture and blend until smooth.
Pour the almond cream into the dish and arrange the orange slices on top. Broil for about 10 minutes.
Leave to cool a little and serve warm.

Almond filling

You will want to dip your finger in this, like a child! You can use it as a base for tarts, especially ones made with cherries or other pit fruit. During cooking the almond cream absorbs the flavour of the fruit and helps to keep the pastry crisp.

Serves 4–6
Preparation time: 10 minutes

1¼ sticks butter, at room temperature, cubed
1 cup confectioners' sugar
3 eggs
1¼ cups ground almonds
½ cup all-purpose flour

Mix the butter and confectioners' sugar together in a large bowl with a whisk. As soon as the mixture turns pale, add the eggs one at a time and stir.
Then pour in the ground almonds, mix well, and add the flour.
The hardest part is done: just keep it in the refrigerator until you want to use it.

Chestnut spread

Sufficient for filling 1 sponge cake or 10 meringues

Preparation time: 10 minutes

10 oz tinned chestnut purée
½ vanilla bean
3–4 tablespoons superfine sugar

Scrape the seeds out of the vanilla bean and discard the husk. Blend the ingredients in a food processor. Chill in the refrigerator until you want to use it. Use to fill a sponge cake or meringues.

Orange and almond gratin

Floating islands

Serves 4–6
Preparation time: 10 minutes
Cooking time: 3 minutes

8 egg whites
1 pinch of salt
custard (see page 18)

Heat a large saucepan of water.
Put the egg whites in a large bowl, add the pinch of salt, and beat with an electric whisk to form stiff peaks.
When the water is boiling, carefully place spoonfuls of egg white in the water. Lower the heat and leave to cook for 3 minutes.
Use a skimmer to lift out the egg whites, drain them, and float them on top of the custard.
You may like to pour a little caramel over the egg whites.

Baked custard

See page 18 for recipe

Egg custard

Serves 4–6
Preparation time: 10 minutes
Cooking time: 30 minutes

1 baking pan

4 cups milk
1 scant cup superfine sugar
1 vanilla bean
6 eggs

Preheat the oven to 300° F.
Put the milk in a heavy-based saucepan with the sugar and vanilla bean, split in two lengthways. Bring to the boil. Whisk the eggs in a large bowl and gradually pour them into the boiling milk, stirring all the time. Then pour the eggs and milk into a mold.
Place the mold in a deep dish two-thirds full of boiling water. Cook in the oven for about 30 minutes.
Serve warm in the dish in which it was cooked.
You can flavor the egg custard with the grated rind of half a lemon.

Table of recipes

Table of recipes

Acknowledgments

A big thanks to Elio, his father and mother, for the photo on page 27 and to Marie-Monique for the use of her house.

Thanks too to Akiko and Pierre for their patience.

For trying out the recipes: Ilona Chovankova

Shopping and household items

Maison de Famille, 10 place de la Madeleine, 75008 Paris
for pages 39 (bowl), 45 (plate, top left), 53 and 71 (plate and cake dish), 77, 84, 97, 101, 119, 121, 131, 139, 140, 146 and 155.

Printed in Singapore by Tien Wah Press